Practical Korean

Your Guide to Speaking Korean Quickly and Effortlessly in a Few Hours

Samuel E. Martin

TUTTLE Publishing

Tokyo | Rutland, Vermont | Singapore

The Tuttle Story: "Books to Span the East and West"

Most people are surprised to learn that the world's largest publisher of books on Asia had its humble beginnings in the tiny American state of Vermont. The company's founder, Charles E. Tuttle, belonged to a New England family steeped in publishing. And his first love was naturally books—especially old and rare editions.

Immediately after WW II, serving in Tokyo under General Douglas MacArthur, Tuttle was tasked with reviving the Japanese publishing industry. He later founded the Charles E. Tuttle Publishing Company, which thrives today as one of the world's leading independent publishers.

Though a westerner, Tuttle was hugely instrumental in bringing a knowledge of Japan and Asia to a world hungry for information about the East. By the time of his death in 1993, Tuttle had published over 6,000 books on Asian culture, history and art—a legacy honored by the Japanese emperor with the "Order of the Sacred Treasure," the highest tribute Japan can bestow upon a non-Japanese.

With a backlist of 1,500 titles, Tuttle Publishing is more active today than at any time in its past—inspired by Charles Tuttle's core mission to publish fine books to span the East and West and provide a greater understanding of each.

Published by Tuttle Publishing, an imprint of Periplus Editions (HK) Ltd.

www.tuttlepublishing.com

Copyright © 2013 Periplus Editions (HK) Ltd

New edition, 2013. Previous editions © 1965 and 2008 by Periplus Editions (HK) Ltd.
All rights reserved.

ISBN 978-0-8048-4344-7

16 15 14 13
6 5 4 3 2 1

Printed in Singapore   1305MP

TUTTLE PUBLISHING® is a registered trademark of Tuttle Publishing, a division of Periplus Editions (HK) Ltd.

Distributed by:

Asia Pacific
Berkeley Books Pte Ltd, 61 Tai Seng Avenue #02-12, Singapore 534167
Tel: (65) 6280 1330; Fax: (65) 6280 6290
inquiries@periplus.com.sg
www.periplus.com

Japan
Tuttle Publishing, Yaekari Building, 3rd Floor, 5-4-12 Osaki,
Shinagawa-ku, Tokyo 141-0032
Tel: (81)3 5437-0171; Fax: (81)3 5437-0755
sales@tuttle.co.jp
www.tuttle.co.jp

North America, Latin America & Europe
Tuttle Publishing, 364 Innovation Drive,
North Clarendon, VT 05759-9436, USA
Tel: 1 (802) 773-8930; Fax: 1 (802) 773 6993
info@tuttlepublishing.com
www.tuttlepublishing.com

Contents

About This Revised Edition

Samuel E. Martin's guide to learning Korean has firmly stood the test of time, as thousands of beginning learners continue to attest; his book has remained continuously in print since its original release in 1954.

It's an extremely useful, compact guide that's especially aimed at tourists and visitors to Korea, and with more people now visiting Korea than ever before, we hope this new revised edition will be greeted with enthusiasm.

This revised edition reflects several improvements, and some of the examples and phrases have been updated to reflect current usage. Korean text (**Hangeul**) is included throughout, and the romanization system follows the Korean government's most recent method.

We hope that *Practical Korean* helps you to succeed with the Korean language, just as it's helped many others.

Introduction

THIS BOOK has been written to fill a specific need: that of the hundreds of thousands of people now visiting Korea for business or holidays, or even living there for a year or two, who wish to learn something of the language spoken around them. The structure of Korean is peculiarly complex, and difficulties plague the foreign student from the very beginning. I have attempted to simplify some of the common problems and to acquaint the reader with the most useful way to say a lot of everyday things, without having to memorize long lists of grammatical rules.

The sentences are almost all given in the Polite (**yo**) style, which is both the simplest and the most widely useful. From this style, another common style—the Intimate style—is easily derived simply by dropping the final particle. Koreans who look at the book will miss the Formal (**-seumnida**) style which they feel more appropriate to use with foreigners on first acquaintance. My purpose in sticking to one style is to provide the reader with the means to say a great many different things, rather than teach him or her a great many ways to say the same thing. From an academic point of view, this approach has certain drawbacks. From a practical point of view, however, it is the quickest and simplest way to put the foreigner into direct communication with Koreans, and that is the aim of this book.

The material is presented using the romanization method that is officially authorized by the Korean government. The equivalents in other romanization systems are given in the table at the very end of this book.

The reader who plans to go on with his or her study of Korean beyond the material contained in this book will probably find it advisable to do so in the native script (**Hangeul**). For a scientific description of the structure of Korean, the reader is referred to the author's other publications, *Korean Phonemics* and *Korean Morphophonemics*.

I hope that the material contained in this book—while perhaps oversimplifying a complicated language—will be of some immediate, practical use to the reader who wants to learn some Korean. And I hope some of those who learn Korean in a hurry will find such an interest in the language and the people who speak it that they will someday spare the time and patience needed to master the language more in depth.

SAMUEL E. MARTIN

LESSON 1

Vowels

The vowels and combinations of **y** or **w** with a vowel are pronounced somewhat as follows:

i		as in mar*i*ne (m*ee*t, ch*ea*t)
	wi	as in *we* (q*uee*n, bet*wee*n, s*wee*t)
e		as in m*e*t (or h*ey*, s*ay*, m*a*te)
	ye	as in *yes* (or *yeah*)
	we	as in *wet* (or *way*, *sway*, *qua*ke)
oe		usually pronounced just like the English word *we*
ae		as *at* (c*a*p, s*a*ck, h*a*m)
	yae	as in *yam*
	wae	as in *swam*
a		as *ah* (father)
	ya	as *yard*, German *ja*
	wa	as *Wah*shington (but not *Wor*shington or *Woh*shington!)
eu		as "*jist*" (= just), "*pirty*" (= pretty); or, as J*u*ne, s*oo*n, t*oo*, c*oo*l (WITH LIPS PULLED BACK HARD)
u		as J*u*ne, s*oo*n, t*oo* (WITH LIPS PUSHED OUT)
	yu	as *you*, c*ue*, p*ew* (WITH LIPS PUSHED OUT)

eo		between s*o*ng and s*u*ng; like s*o*ng, l*a*w, b*ough*t (WITH LIPS PULLED BACK HARD); or like s*u*ng, l*u*ng, b*u*tt (WITH TONGUE PULLED BACK AND PUSHED DOWN, AS IF WITH A SPOON)
	yeo	between *yaw*n and *you*ng
	wo	between *wa*ll and *wo*n
o		as in n*o*
	yo	as in y*o*kel

ui   The combination **ui** has three different pronunciations depending on the usage:

(1) At the beginning of a word it is pronounced like **u**.

(2) At the end of a word it is pronounced like **i**.

(3) As a separate particle meaning *of*, it is pronounced like **e**.

In this book, you will find the first pronunciation indicated as **ui(i)** and the second as **eu i**. But you will have to remember that the particle **ui** is pronounced like **e**.

Here are some common words to practice the vowels on:

i	tooth	이
jip	house	집
gwi	ear	귀
jwi	rat	쥐
dwi	behind	뒤
ne	yes	네
ye	yes	예
gyohoe	church	교회
hoeui	meeting	회의
Choe	Choe (name)	최
soe	iron	쇠
sae	bird	새
sonyeo	girl	소녀
agi	baby	아기
hae	sun, year	해

maeil	every day	매일
iyagi	story, talk	이야기
wae	why	왜
mal	horse	말
bam	night	밤
joreugi	badger; tighten	조르기
wanbyeok	perfect, perfection	완벽
gwanggo	advertisement	광고
eumsik	food	음식
eunhaeng	bank	은행
geurim	picture	그림
nun	eye; snow	눈
mu	turnip	무
yuri	glass	유리
dubu	bean-curd, tofu	두부
gyuyul	regulations	규율
meonjeo	first of all	먼저
eonje	when	언제
neomu mani	too much	너무 많이
gyeogjehak	economics	경제학
geokjjeong	worry	걱정
won	won (currency)	원
ssaum	quarrel	싸움
don	money	돈
sori	sound	소리
gong	ball	공
pyo	ticket	표
hakgyo	school	학교
uija	chair	의자
uisa	doctor	의사
uimi	meaning	의미
jipjung	attention	집중
uinon	discussion	의논

LESSON 2

Consonants

The consonants **m**, **n**, and **h** are pronounced much like in English.

The consonant written **ng** is pronounced as in si*ng*, si*ng*er (but NOT as in English fi*ng*er which sounds like fi*ngg*er).

The consonants **b**, **d**, and **g** sound like weakly articulated English *p*in, *t*in, *k*in; but at the end of a syllable (hi*p*, hi*t*, hic*k*) be careful not to give these consonants a special release—just shut the sound off.

The sounds written **p**, **t** and **k** are said with a heavy puff of breath like English u*ph*eaval, pen*th*ouse, coo*kh*ouse.

The sounds written **pp**, **tt**, and **kk** are pronounced with the throat and mouth muscles very tense and released sharp with no puff of breath, a little like English *sp*y, *st*ay, *sk*id.

B, **d**, and **g** are LAX; **p**, **t**, and **k** are BREATHY; and **pp**, **tt**, and **kk** are TENSE. In the same way **j** is lax (as in English *ch*urch weakly articulated), **ch** is breathy (as in English bea*ch h*ouse), and **jj** is tense.

You may hear **pp**, **tt**, **kk**, and **jj** like English *b*it, *d*ip, *g*o, and *J*oe—if you pronounce these words with a specially strong emphasis. But ordinarily English *b*, *d*, *g*, and *j* are rather weakly pronounced like the way Korean **b**, **d**, **g**, and **j** sound between voiced sounds.

The Korean sound **s** is lax and sounds like a very weak English *s*—or, sometimes, especially in front of the vowel **i**, like English *sh*. The Korean sound **ss** is tense and sounds like a very emphatic English *s*. Don't worry if you can't hear the difference between these two; there are few situations in which you will be misunderstood if you confuse them.

The Korean sound which we write sometimes **l** and sometimes **r** is very difficult for Americans because it sounds like a number of different English sounds. Within a word when it sounds like the *l* in fi*ll* we write it **l**; when it sounds like the *r* in British be*rr*y (or the *t* in English Be*tt*y; or the Japanese *r*, or the single Spanish *r*) we write it **r**. Be careful to pronounce the Korean **mm**, **nn**, and **ll** as DOUBLE sounds: like English ge*m-ma*ker, pe*n-kn*ife we*ll-li*ked.

Here are some common words to practice the consonants.

bi	rain	비
pi	blood	피
maekju	beer	맥주
byeo	rice plant	벼
pyo	ticket	표
ppyeo	bone	뼈
dal	moon	달
tal	mask	탈
ttal	daughter	딸
do	province	도
top	a saw	톱
tto	again, yet	또
gi	spirit, disposition	기
ki	height, size	키
kki	a meal	끼
gae	dog	개
kal	knife	칼
kkae	sesame	깨
jo	millet	조
cho	candle	초
jjok	side, direction	쪽
sal	flesh	살
ssal	uncooked rice	쌀
seoda	stands up	서다
sseuda	writes	쓰다
dambae	cigarettes	담배
gongbu	study	공부
Ilbon	Japan	일본

yeoseot beon	six times	여섯 번
chimdae	bed	침대
bando	peninsula	반도
dalda	is sweet	달다
chuptta	is cold	춥다
jaktta	is small	작다
Yeongguk	England	영국
gwail	fruit	과일
sipgu	nineteen	십구
namja	man, male	남자
hwanja	patient	환자
maekju	beer	맥주
jongi	paper	종이
dongan	interval; baby face	동안
iri	this way	이리
geureoke	in that way, so	그렇게
leseutorang	restaurant	레스토랑
ladio	radio	라디오
piryo	necessity	필요
parwol	August	팔월
il	work, job	일
mul	water	물
mullon	of course	물론
ppalli	fast	빨리

Sound Changes

When you link words together without pausing between, certain sound changes take place. If the first word ends in a consonant and the second begins with a vowel, the final consonant of the first word is pronounced as the initial consonant of the second word:

			NOTE PRONUNCIATION CHANGE
seom-i	섬이	island (as subject)	**= seo mi**
seom-e	섬에	to the island	**= seo me**

If the final consonant is **p, t, ch,** or **k** it changes in sound to **b, d, j,** or **g**:

			NOTE PRONUNCIATION CHANGE
chaek-i	책이	book (as subject)	**chae gi**
hanguk-e	한국에	to Korea	**Hangu ge**
bap-i	밥이	cooked rice (as subject)	**ba bi**
naj-e	낮에	in the daytime	**na je**

If the final consonant is **l**, it changes in sound to **r**:

			NOTE PRONUNCIATION CHANGE
il-i	일이	work (as subject)	**= i ri**
mul-eul	물을	water (as object)	**= mu reul**

If the second word begins with **m** or **n** and the first word ends in **p**, **t**, or **k**, these change to **m**, **n**, and **ng** respectively:

			NOTE PRONUNCIATION CHANGE
jib mada	집마다	every house	**jim mada**
mot meok kko	못먹고	can't eat	**mon meok kko**
chaek mada	책마다	every book	**chaeng mada**

The combinations **tp**, **ts**, and **tk** usually sound like **pp**, **ss**, and **kk**:

			NOTE PRONUNCIATION CHANGE
mot bwayo	못봐요	can't see	**mo ppwayo**
mot sayo	못사요	can't buy	**mo ssayo**
mot gayo	못가요	can't go	**mo kkayo**

At the end of a word before a pause or another consonant, the only consonants which occur are **p**, **t**, **k**, **m**, **n**, **ng**, and **l**. But there are a few words which have basic forms (the forms you hear when linked with a following word beginning with a vowel) in other consonant combinations. These are changed as follows (see also Lesson 16):

BEFORE VOWEL		BEFORE PAUSE OR CONSONANT
P		**P**
ape 앞에	in front	**ap** front; **apdo** front too
PS		**P**
gapsi 값이	price (subj.)	**kap** price; **kapdo** price too
S		**T**
oseul 옷을	clothes (object)	**ot** clothes; **otdo** clothes too

BEFORE VOWEL		BEFORE PAUSE OR CONSONANT
N		**N**
jeong woneun 정원은	garden (topic)	**jeongwon** garden; **jeongwon do** garden too
CH **kkocheun** 꽃은	flower (topic)	**T** **kkot** flower; **kkotdo** flower too
J **naje** 낮에	in the daytime	**T** **nat** daytime; **natdo** daytime too
KK **bakke** 밖에	outside	**K** **bak** outside; **bakdo** outside too
LG **dalgi** 닭이	chicken (subj.)	**K** **dak** chicken; **dakdo** chicken too

There are certain other sound changes which are less regular. You may also notice sound variants. Sometimes the same thing will be pronounced in two different ways even by the same speaker. The most common of these is the dropping of **h** between voiced sounds:

man(h)i	lots	많이
bang(h)ak	school vacation	방학
a(h)op	nine	아홉
pyeong(h)waropkke	peacefully	평화롭게
eun(h)aeng	bank	은행

You may also notice that **w** sometimes drops, especially after **b**, **p**, **pp**, **m**, **u**, **o**:

WRITTEN AS:			PRONOUNCED AS:
jeomwon	clerk	점원	**jeomeon**
Guwol	September	구월	**Gueol**
Samwol	March	삼월	**Sameol**
Owol	May	오월	**Oeol**

One irregular sound change which is quite common is the replacement of an initial **b**, **d**, **j**, **s**, or **g** by their tense counterparts **pp**, **tt**, **jj**, **ss**, or **kk**. In this book, the "reinforcement" of the initial sound is sometimes shown with parentheses: **(p)p**, **(t)t**, **(j)j**, **(s)s**, or **(k)k**. For example:

WRITTEN AS:			PRONOUNCED AS:
eojetbam	last night	어젯밤	**eojetppam**
yeoldul	twelve	열둘	**yeolttul**

NOTE: It is important to remember that **b**, **d**, **j**, **g**, and **r** are just positional variants of **p**, **t**, **ch**, **k**, and **l** respectively. **B** and **p** function as one sound unit in the structure of Korean and the native script (**Hangeul**) writes both with the same symbol. This is true also for **d** and **t**, **j**, and **ch**, **g** and **k**, **r** and **l** respectively. So when we speak of an ending beginning with **t**, it goes without saying we mean to add "(and this changes to **d** automatically between voiced sounds)."

LESSON 4

Names and Greetings

Annyeong haseyo?
안녕하세요? (Literally it means, are you well?)
How are you? / Hello.

Gomapseumnida.
고맙습니다.
Thank you.

Joesong hamnida.
죄송합니다.
My apologies, I'm sorry.

Mian hamnida.
미안합니다.
I'm sorry.

Sillye haesseumnida.
실례했습니다.
Excuse me (for something I did).

Sillye hamnida.
실례합니다.
Excuse me (for something I am doing).

Sillye hagesseumnida.
실례하겠습니다.
Excuse me (for something I am going to do).

Cheonman eyo.
천만에요.
(It's one in 10 million words =) Not at all. Think nothing of it.

Gwaen chan seumnikka?
괜찮습니까?
Is it all right? May I?
or
Josseumnikka?
좋습니까?
Is it all right? May I? (more polite expression)

Gwaen chan seumnida.
괜찮습니다.
It makes no difference; it's OK; you may.

Josseumnida.
좋습니다.
It's all right; it's good; it's fine: you may.

Eoseo deureoosipsio.
어서 들어오십시요.
Come right in.

Tto boepgesseumnida.
또 뵙겠습니다.
See you later. So long.

Pyeonhage mani deuseyo.
편하게 많이 드세요.
Please help yourself.

Pyeonhage iseuseyo.
편하게 있으세요.
Please make yourself at home.

An nyeong(h)i gasipsio.
안녕히 가십시요.
Goodbye (to one who is leaving).

Annyeong(h)i gyesipsio.
안녕히 계십시오.
Goodbye (to one who is staying).

A Korean has two names: the family name is followed by a personal name. Most of the family names are of one syllable like **Gim, Bak, Baek, Choe, Jang, Min, Yu, Im,** but a few unusual ones have two syllables like **Hwangbo.** If the family name has one syllable, the personal name has two: **I Seung man** (Syngman Rhee). **Gim Il(s)seong** (Kim Ilsung). This system, together with most of the names themselves, was borrowed from China. Some names are exceptions to this system.

The word **seonsaeng** has two meanings: one is *teacher*, the other is a title which can be translated *Mr., Mrs.,* or *Miss* depending on whom you are talking about. There is a word for *you* (**dangsin**) but instead of using it the Koreans usually refer to a person either by title and name: **Gim seonsaeng** = *You* (, *Mr. Kim*), or just by title: **seonsaeng** = *You* (, *sir*). To make this more polite the word **nim** is often added: **seonsaengnim.**

The word for *I, me* is **na**; for *my* **nae.** For *he* or *she* you say **geusaram** or **geui** = *that person,* for *his* or *hers* you say **geu saram-ui** or just **geu** = *of that person.* For *they, them* you can say either **geusaram** or **geu saramdeul.** For *their* **geu saram-ui** or **geu saramdeul-ui. Uri** means *we* or *our* but sometimes it translates into English *me* or *my.*

You will notice that many common expressions have meanings which seem different from their literal translations. These literal translations are intended only as a help in remembering the words in the expressions.

LESSON 5

Sentence Structure

English sentences seem to tell you a lot more about a given situation than their equivalents in Korean. That is because the Korean likes to leave out any details that seem obvious from the context or the situation. It's a rare English sentence that has no subject, but we use such sentences in postcards (*Having a fine time. Wish you were here.*) and in commands (*Keep off the grass. Send more money.*). In Korean it is quite common to omit the subject, and often many other parts of the equivalent English sentence, too. You'll often wonder why the Korean words for *some, any, it* and other common little English expressions seldom appear in the Korean versions of examples.

A Korean sentence is quite complete with nothing but a verb:

Hamnida.
합니다.
(Someone) does (something).

The subject and object may simply be implied. If the Korean wants to supply further details about the situation, he puts them in before the verb. For example, if he wants to tell just what kind of an action the "does" refers to:

Gongbu hamnida.
공부합니다.
(Someone) does STUDYING = studies (something).

If it seems important to add the object of the action:

Hangungmal-eul gongbu hamnida.
한국말을 공부합니다.
(Someone) studies KOREAN.

And the place:
Hakgyo-eseo Hangungmal-eul gongbu hamnida.
학교에서 한국말을 공부합니다.
(Someone) studies Korean IN SCHOOL.

And the time:
Jigeum hakgyo-eseo Hangungmal-eul gongbu hamnida.
지금 학교에서 한국말을 공부합니다.
(Someone) studies Korean in school NOW.

And the subject of the action (the actor):
Haksaeng-i jigeum hakgyo-eseo Hangungmal-eul gongbu hamnida.
학생이 지금 학교에서 한국말을 공부합니다.
THE STUDENT studies Korean in school now.

The order in which you put the additional information like object, place, time, and subject depends largely on the importance of the information. The indispensable news in every sentence is the verb—this goes at the end. As a general rule, the farther you get away from the end of the sentence, the more dispensable the information you are supplying.

In other words, if you wanted to say the same thing a little more briefly, you'd likely chop off the earlier parts of the sentence first. Since sometimes the SUBJECT is so well known you don't have to mention it, but at other times it's the OBJECT—or the place, or the time, or something else—there isn't any fixed order. If all other things are equal—that is, if you're equally in the dark about subject and object—it's usually better to keep the object near the verb.

Some Useful Expressions

Asigesseumnikka?
아시겠습니까?
Do you understand?
or
Ihae hasigesseumnikka?
이해하시겠습니까?
Do you understand?

Ne.
네.
Yes. (Often pronounced **ye** in the South.)

Ani.
아니.
No.

Aniyo.
아니요.
No. (More polite)

Amnida.
압니다.
I understand.

Moreumnida.
모릅니다.
I don't understand.

Dasi mal hae juseyo.
다시 말해 주세요.
Please say it again.

Cheoncheon(h)i mal hae juseyo.
천천히 말해 주세요.
Please say it slowly.

Chaek-eul boseyo.
책을 보세요.
Please look at your book.

Chaek-eul boji maseyo.
책을 보지 마세요.
Please don't look at your book.

Hangungmal-lo haseyo.
한국말로 하세요.
Please talk in Korean.

Yeongeo-ro mal haji maseyo.
영어로 말하지 마세요.
Please don't talk in English.

Gachi hapsida.
같이 합시다.
Let's do it (say it) together.

Da gachi.
다 같이.
All together.

Deutgi-man haseyo.
듣기만 하세요.
Just listen please.

Geureosseumnikka?
그렇습니까?
Is that so? Oh? Really?

(Or, the more casual expression:)
Geurae(yo)?
그래(요)?
Is it? Is that so? Oh, really?

Geureosseumnida.
그렇습니다.
That's so. Yes. That's it.

Geureochiman....
그렇지만....
But.... However....

Geurigo....
그리고....
And (in addition)....

Geuraeseo....
그래서....
And so.... So....

....gatta jusipsio.
갖다 주십시오.
Please bring me....

More Useful Expressions

Ppalli gaseyo.
빨리 가세요.
Please go fast.

Cheoncheon(h)i gaseyo.
천천히 가세요.
Please go slow.

Oreunjjok-euro.
오른쪽으로.
To the right.

Oenjjok-euro.
왼쪽으로.
To the left.

Gojjang ap-euro.
곧장 앞으로.
Straight ahead.

Yeogi.
여기.
Here (near me or us). This place.

Jeogi.
저기.
Over there (away from you and me). That place over there.

Iri-ro.
이리로.
This way.

Geuri-ro.
그리로.
That way.

Jeori-ro.
저리로.
That way over there.

Iri-ro osipsio.
이리로 오십시오.
Please come this way.

Igeo(t).
이거 (이것)
This (thing).

Geugeo(t).
그것.
That (thing).

Jeogeo(t).
저거 (저것)
That (thing) over there.

Eodi?
어디.
Where? What place?

M(u)eo(t)?
뭐   뭣   무어   무엇?
What? (Pronounced **mueot**, **mueo**, **meot**, or **meo**.)

Wae?
왜?
Why?

Eonje?
언제?
When?

Jigeum.
지금.
Now. (Also pronounced **Jikkeum**.)

Oneul.
오늘.
Today.

Naeil.
내일.
Tomorrow.

Eoje.
어제.
Yesterday.

I daeum-e.
이 다음에.
Next (after this).

Geu daeum-e.
그 다음에.
Next (after that).

Najung-e.
나중에.
Later (after this).

Geu hu-e.
그 후에.
Later (after that).

Geu jeon-e.
그 전에.
Before that.

Beolsseo.
벌써.
Already.

Ajik.
아직.
Not yet.

Jogeum.
조금.
A little. (Also pronounced **Jjokkeum** and **Jjogeum**.)

Jom deo.
좀 더.
A little more. (Also pronounced **Jjom deo**.)

Deo mani.
더 많이.
More.

Jogeum man juseyo.
조금 만 주세요.
Give me a little please.

Jogeum deo juseyo.
조금 더 주세요.
Please give me a little more.

Jomcheoreom.
좀처럼.
Seldom.

Jaju.
자주.
Often.

Neomu.
너무.
Too much.

Chungbun(h)i.
충분히.
Enough.

Mani.
많이.
Lots.

Da.
다.
All.

Jal.
잘.
(1) Well. (2) Lots. (3) Often.

Cham.
참.
Really. Very. Quite.

"Is" and "Has"

There are two verbs which translate the English word *is, am, are, be* in Korean: **isseoyo** *exists, stays* and **ieyo** *equals*. You use **ieyo** when you have a sentence which can be reduced to the formula A = *B*:

A = B   A   B   =
This IS **a** book.   **Igeo, chaek   ieyo.**

Notice that the formula has to change in Korean because the verb always comes at the end. The verb expression **ieyo** is peculiar in a number of ways: (1) It always has something in front of it, with which it is linked in pronunciation. (Other verbs can make a complete sentence by themselves.) (2) It drops the vowel **i** after a word ending in a vowel.

Geugeon japji eyo.
그건 잡지에요.
That is a magazine.

Gicha eyo.
기차에요.
(It)'s a train.

Mwo eyo?
뭐에요?
What is (it)?

Bihaenggi eyo.
비행기에요.
It's an airplane.

Nugu eyo?
누구에요?
Who is it?

Jeo eyo.
저에요.
It's me.

Geu saram, nugu eyo?
그 사람 누구 에요?
Who is that person? Who is he?

I saram, nae chingu eyo.
이 사람 내 친구에요.
This person is my friend.

Hakgyo seonsaengnim ieyo.
학교 선생님이에요.
He's a school teacher.

Hanguk (s)saram ieyo?
한국 사람이에요?
Is he a Korean (person)?

Aniyo. Miguk (s)saram ieyo.
아니요. 미국 사람 이에요.
No. He's an American (person).

Yeogi eodi eyo?
여기 어디에요?
What place is this place?

Jeogi cheoldoyeok ieyo.
저기 철도역 이에요.
(That place) over there is a railroad station.

Gonghang-i, eodi eyo?
공항이 어디에요?
Where (what place) is the airport?

Jeogi eyo.
저기에요.
It's (that place) over there.

Whenever *is* refers merely to EXISTENCE or to LOCATION rather than to IDENTIFICATION, you use **isseoyo**.

Don(-i), isseoyo?
돈 있어요?
Is there any money?

Eodi isseoyo?
어디있어요?
Where is it?

Jungguk (s)saram(-i), eodi isseoyo?
중국 사람이 어디있어요?
Where's the Chinese (person)?

This is the ordinary way of saying *has* or *got*: I've got a cat. = There exists a cat.

Goyangi-ga isseoyo.
고양이가 있어요.
(Someone) has a cat.

Kim seon saeng, jadongcha(-ga) isseoyo?
김 선생 자동차(가) 있어요?
Do you have a car, Mr. Kim?

Aniyo. Jajeongeo-man isseoyo.
아니요. 자전거만 있어요.
No, I have only a bicycle.

To say *does not have* or *hasn't got* you use the verb expression **eopseoyo**:

Sigan(-i) eopseoyo.
시간(이) 없어요.
There isn't time = I haven't any time.

Don(-i) eopseoyo.
돈(이) 없어요
I haven't any money.

Sige(-ga) eopseoyo?
시계(가) 없어요?
Haven't you got a watch (clock)?

Ai(-ga) eopseoyo?
아이(가) 없어요?
Don't you have any children?

LESSON 9

Styles of Speech

Each Korean sentence can be said in many different ways, depending on who is talking to whom. In America, even if you divide the people up into regular folks and snobs, you still talk much the same way to anyone. But a Korean uses different verb forms at the end of his or her sentence for different people he or she talks to. The system is quite complicated, and as a foreigner you won't be expected to get the hang of it right away.

In this book most of the sentences are in the POLITE or **yo** style, because this is the simplest to learn, and it is also the most generally useful. Some of the sentences, especially set greetings, are given in the FORMAL or **-seumnida** style.

Since you will hear a lot of the other styles, too, you had better know a little about them. In some of the styles there are different endings depending on whether your sentence is a STATEMENT, QUESTION, COMMAND or PROPOSITION. But in others, like the polite style, these are all the same, and you show the difference by intonation.

In making a command or proposition, Koreans often use the formal style even though they would ordinarily be talking to the person in the polite style—it's like adding *"please"* in English. On the next page is a list of some of the endings characteristic of the various styles.

The use of these styles is somewhat like this. You use the *formal* style to persons of higher status than you, and also to other people in formal situations. To strangers, you use the formal style until the ice is broken—after that, the polite style.

You use the *intimate* style (which is just the polite style with the polite particle **yo** dropped) with close friends and relatives, often mixing it with plain style.

You use the *plain* style in talking to children, and sometimes with close friends and relatives. You use the *quotation* style (which is almost identical with the plain) when you are quoting what someone has said; or when writing an article or book.

The *familiar* or "buddy-buddy" style is used among friends.

The *authoritative* style is used by a person taking command of a situation: a policeman to a traffic offender, a customer to a delivery person, a guest to a hotel clerk, a passenger in a taxi. But should you be in any of these situations you certainly won't cause any hard feelings by using the polite style.

STYLE	STATEMENT	QUESTION	COMMAND	PROPOSITION
Formal	**-seumnida**	**-seumnikka**		
	-eumnida	**-eumnikka**	**-hasipsio**	**-hasipsida**
	-mnida	**-mnikka**	**-sipsio**	**-sipsida**
Plain	**-da**	**-ni**	**-haera**	**-haja**
	-nhada			
Quotation	AS ABOVE	**-neunya**	**-eura**	AS ABOVE
Familiar	**-ne**	**-na**	**-ge (na)**	**-se**
Authoritative	**-so**			
	-eu		**-eusio**	**-eupsida**
	-o		**-sio**	**-psida**
Intimate	**-eo, -a, -e, -ae**			
Polite	**-eoyo, -ayo, -eyo, -aeyo**			

Speech styles are quite different from "honorifics," discussed in Lesson 25.

See if you can identify the style of each of the following utterances just by their endings. Don't memorize the sentences:

Bi-ga wasseumnikka?
비가 왔습니까?
Did it rain?

Yeogi-seo Jungguk eumsik-eul meogeulsu isseoyo?
여기서 중국음식을 먹을 수 있어요?
Can I eat (= be served) Chinese food here?

Naeil olgeyo.
내일 올게요.
I'll come back tomorrow.

Bang-i eopseoyo?
방이 없어요?
Haven't you a (vacant) room?

Eonje onayo?
언제 오나요
When did you get here?

Jamkkan shwipsida.
잠깐 쉽시다.
Let's rest a minute.

Yeogi anjara.
여기 앉아라.
Sit here.

Igeot boseyo.
이것 보세요.
Look at this.

Ppalli gaseyo.
빨리 가세요
Please go fast.

Jip-e oseyo.
집에 오세요.
Come to (my) house.

Mwo hani?
뭐 하니?
What are you doing?

Gachi haja.
같이 하자.
Let's do it together.

Jigeum moegeosseoyo.
지금 먹었어요.
I've just now eaten.

Geu chaek-eul beolsseo ilgeosseoyo?
그 책을 벌써 읽었어요?
Have you already seen (or read) that book?

Iri wa.
이리와.
Come this way.

Pyeonghwa-ga olkkayo?
평화가 올까요?
Will peace come?

Geu-neun gongbu-reul yeolsim(h)i handa.
그는 공부를 열심히 한다.
He studies hard.

Geu goyangi-neun yeppeuda.
그 고양이는 예쁘다.
The cat is pretty.

Neomu jakda.
너무 작다.
It's too small.

Keumnikka?

큽니까?

Is it large?

Yeoboseyo.

여보세요.

Hello. (when answering a phone call)

Yeogiyo.

여기요.

Look, excuse me... (Literally means, here)

Some Handy Nouns

Korean nouns occur in four different types of construction:

(1) Followed by a PARTICLE (Lessons 12, 13, 14) which shows the grammatical relationship of the noun to the rest of the sentence—whether it is the subject or object or place of the action.

Hakgyo-ga keoyo.
학교가 커요.
The school is big.

Hakgyo-reul bwayo.
학교를 봐요.
I see the school.

Hakgyo-eseo gongbu haeyo.
학교에서 공부해요.
I study at school.

(2) Followed by the verb **ieyo** *equals*: is (Lesson 8) as the B part of the formula (A) = B.

(Geu jip) hakgyo eyo.   That (building) is a school.

(3) Before another noun or a noun phrase which it modifies (describes).

Hakgyo seonsaeng.
학교 선생.
A school teacher.

(4) All by itself, in an absolute construction, usually followed by a pause.

Hakgyo-ka eodi isseoyo?
학교가 어디 있어요?
Where is there a school?

Hakgyo gaseyo?
학교 가세요?
Are you going to school?

A Korean noun like **chaek** = *book* means all of these: *a book, some books, any books, the books*. You usually have to tell from the context whether the noun is plural, definite, or whatnot. There is a plural indicator **deul** = *group* often added at the end of a noun or noun phrase, but you can't count on it. **Chaek deul** means *books* but then so does **chaek** all by itself.

Here are some handy common nouns:

yeonpil	pencil	연필
jongi	paper	종이
sinmun	newspaper	신문
dambae	cigarette	담배
gabang	briefcase, suitcase, handbag	가방
gongchaek	notebook	공책
jip	house, building	집
maejeom	stand, small shop	매점
sangjeom	store	상점
jang, sijang	market	장, 시장
ucheguk	post office	우체국
eumsikjeom	restaurant	음식점
gongjang	factory	공장

samusil	office	사무실
sang	table	상
chaeksang	desk	책상
uija	chair	의자
hwajangsil	toilet	화장실
jumeoni	pocket	주머니
bul	fire	불
mul	water	물
sul	liquor	술
binu	soap	비누
sugeon	towel	수건
utdori	shirt	웃도리
baji	trousers	바지
yangmal	socks	양말
gudu	dress shoes	구두
sinbal	shoes	신발
jaket	overcoat	자켓, 코트
moja	hat	모자
keompyuteo	computer	컴퓨터
hyudaepon /	cell phone	휴대폰/핸드폰
haendeupon		
gonghang	airport	공항
taeksi	taxi	택시
hotel	hotel	호텔
namja	man, boy	남자
yoeja	woman, girl	여자
chima	skirt	치마

More Handy Nouns

Hanguk	Korea	한국
Bukhan	North Korea	북한
Namhan	South Korea	남한
Jungguk	China	중국
Leosia	Russia	러시아
Ilbon	Japan	일본
Miguk	America	미국
Dogil	Germany	독일
Kaenada	Canada	캐나다
Hoju	Australia	호주
Taeguk	Thailand	태국
Indo	India	인도
Yureop	Europe	유럽
Yeongguk	England	영국
Nyujillaedeu	New Zealand	뉴질랜드
Singgapol	Singapore	싱가폴
Malleijia	Malaysia	말레이지아
Dongnam-Asia	Southeast Asia	동남아시아
Daeman	Taiwan	대만
Beteunam	Vietnam	베트남
Peurangseu	France	프랑스
Italia	Italy	이탈리아
Asia	Asia	아시아
jeomwon	clerk (in store)	점원
sawon	clerk (in office)	사원
nampyeon	husband	남편

an(h)ae	(one's own wife)	아내
buin	(someone else's wife)	부인

LESSON 12

Particles

A PARTICLE is a little word which shows the relationship between the word or phrase preceding it and the rest of the sentence. Some Korean particles are similar in function to English prepositions (*in, on, at, from, till, of*); others indicate grammatical relationships which English shows by word order—like subject and object.

In English it makes a difference whether we say *The cat eats the bird* or *The bird eats the cat*. But in Korean the *cat* (**goyangi**) and the *bird* (**sae**) can come in either order with either meaning: **goyangi, sae, meogeoyo** means either *The cat eats the bird* or *The bird eats the cat*. And both meanings hold for **sae, goyangi, meogeoyo** too.

The order in which we put the two nouns is determined by EMPHASIS rather than by which one does the eating. In order to make it clear which is the SUBJECT (which one eats) and which is the OBJECT (which one gets eaten), Korean uses different particles:

Goyangi-ga sae-reul meogeoyo and **Sae-reul goyangi-ga meogeoyo** both mean *The cat eats the bird*. **Sae-ga goyangi-reul meogeoyo** and also **Goyangi-reul sae-ga meogeoyo** both mean *The bird eats the cat*.

One characteristic of a particle is that you practically never pause in front of it—it's always linked with the preceding word.

There are TWO-SHAPE particles and ONE-SHAPE particles. The one-shape particles always look the same, regardless of the word they follow. The two-shape particles have different shapes depending on the shape of the preceding word.

MEANING OF PARTICLE	SHAPE AFTER CONSONANT	SHAPE AFTER VOWEL
subject	**i**	**ga**
object	**eul**	**reul**
"with, and"	**gwa**	**wa**
"or, and"	**ina**	**na**
polite style	**iyo**	**yo**
"hey!, Oh!" (vocative)	**a**	**ya**

Here are some examples with words of the preceding lessons:

PARTICLE	AFTER CONSONANT	AFTER VOWEL
subject	**ireum-i** 이름이	**dambae-ga** 담배가
	bang-i 방이	**nai-ga** 나이가
	mul-i (mu-ri) 물이	**binu-ga** 비누가
object	**yangmal-eul** 양말을	**gudu-reul** 구두를
	sinmun-eul 신문을	**jongi-reul** 종이를
	sangjeom-eul 상점을	**hakgyo-reul** 학교를
"with, and"	**hyeong-gwa*** 형과	**na wa** 나와
	gajok-gwa* 가족과	**chingu-wa** 친구와
	Iut-gwa* 이웃과	**nongbu-wa** 농부와
"or, and, or the like"	**sugeon-ina** 수건이나	**baj-ina** 바지나

* Don't forget **k** sounds like **g** between voiced sounds.

PARTICLE	AFTER CONSONANT	AFTER VOWEL
	chaeksang-ina 책상이나	**moja-na** 모자나
polite style	**Seonsaengnim iyo!** 선생님이요 (You!)	**Nuguyo?** 누구요 (Who?)
vocative	**Gim seonsaeng!** 김 선생 (Oh, Mr. Kim!)	**Gim moksa!** 김 목사 (Oh, Reverend Kim!)
	Gildong a! 길동아 (Hey, Poktong!)	**Yeongsu ya!** 영수야 (Hey, Haksu!)

NOTE: Before the subject particle, the following nouns have different shapes:

na	I	나	**nae-ga**	내가
je	I (formal)	제	**je-ga**	제가
nugu	who	누구	**nu-ga**	누가

LESSON 13

More Particles

Here are some one-shape particles, with examples after both consonants and vowels:

PARTICLE	MEANINGS	EXAMPLES
ui (PRO-NOUNCED **e**)	modification or subordination	**Gim seonsaeng-ui chaek ieyo.** 김선생의 책이에요 It's Mr. Kim's book. **Nugu-ui moja eyo?** 누구의 모자에요? Whose hat is it?
e	(1) direction *to*	**Geu-neun hakgyo-e gamnida.** 그는 학교에 갑니다 He goes to school. **Geu-neun eun(h)aeng-e gamnida.** 그는 은행에 갑니다. He goes to the bank.
	(2) location *at, in*	**Geu-neun hakgyo-e isseoyo.** 그는 학교에 있어요. He is in school. **Geu-neun eun(h)aeng-e isseoyo.** 그는 은행에 있어요. He's at the bank.

PARTICLE	MEANINGS	EXAMPLES
	(3) a point in time *at, in*	**Han si-e ol geyo.** 한 시에 올게요. I'm coming at one o'clock. **Ojeon-e ol geyo.** 오전에 올게요. I'm coming in the morning.
	(4) impersonal indirect object	**Geu reul eun(h)aeng-e bonael geyo.** 그를 은행에 보낼게요. I'm sending (him, it) to the bank. **Hoesa-e pyeonji-reul sseugo isseoyo.** 회사에 편지를 쓰고 있어요. I'm writing a letter to the company.
hante	personal indirect object *to, at, for* (a person)	**Pumonim-hante bonael geyo.** 부모님께 보낼꺼에요. I'm sending it to (my) parents. **Chingu-hante pyeonji-reul sseugo isseoyo.** 친구한테 편지를 쓰고 있어요. I'm writing a letter to my friend.
ege	SAME; less colloquial	**Biseo-ege jul geyo.** 비서에게 줄게요. I'm giving it to the secretary.
bogo	SAME; more colloquial	**Nug-bogo mal hae yo?** 누구보고 말해요? Who are you telling (to)? **Gim seonsaeng-bogo iri ora haseyo.** 김 선생 보고 이리 오라 하세요. Tell Mr. Kim to come here.

PARTICLE	MEANINGS	EXAMPLES
seo, eseo	(1) dynamic location (happens) *at, in*	**Hakkyo-eseo yeongeo-reul baewosseoyo.** 학교에서 영어 배웠어요. I learned English at school. **Seoul-eseo taeeonasseoyo.** 서울에서 태어났어요. I was born in Seoul.
	(2) *from* (a place)	**Yeogi-seo meoreoyo.** 여기서 멀어요. It's far from here. **Ucheguk-eseo oreunjjok-euro doragaseyo.** 우체국에서 오른쪽으로 돌아 가세요. From the post office, turn to the right.
egeseo	*from* (a person)	**Nugu-e ke seo deureosseoyo.** 누구에게서 들었어요. I heard it from someone.
buteo	*from* (a time or place)	**Yeogi-buteo sijak hapsida.** 여기부터 시작합시다. Let's start from here. **Achim-buteo bam-kkaji ilman hamnida.** 아침부터 밤까지 일합니다. I work from morning till night.
kkaji	(all the way up) *to* (a place or time)	**Han si-kkaji oseyo.** 한 시까지 오세요. Come by 1 o'clock. **Yeogi-kkaji hapsida.** 여기까지 합시다. Let's stop here.

PARTICLE	MEANINGS	EXAMPLES
hago	*with, and* (MORE COLLOQUIAL THAN **wa/gwa**)	**Chaek-hago yeonpil kkeonaeseyo.** 책하고 연필 꺼내세요. Take out a book and a pencil. **Chingu-hago gayo.** 친구하고 가요. I'm going (together) with a friend.
man	*just, only*	**Yeonpil-man isseoyo.** 연필만 있어요. I've only got a pencil. **Chingu-man mannayo.** 친구만 만나요. I'm only seeing my friend.
gachi	*like*	**Agi-gachi malhaeyo.** 아기 같이 말해요. He speaks like a baby. **Nabi-kachi chumchwoyo.** 나비같이 춤춰요 She dances like a butterfly.
bak-ke (or **bakke**)	*outside of, except for, aside from, or* (anything) *but*	**Jip-bak-e eopseoyo.** 집 밖에 없어요. I haven't but my house. = I have only my house. (**Jip-man iseoyo.** 집만 있어요.) **Gim moksa-bakke amudo an wasseoyo.** 김목사 밖에 아무도 안 왔어요. (They) didn't come but Rev. Kim = Only Rev. Kim came. (**Kim moksa-man wasseoyo.** 김목사 만 왔어요.)

Some Tricky Particles

The 2-shape particle **euro/ro** has the shape **ro** after vowels, and **euro** after all consonants except **l**; after **l** the shape is **lo: gi ch'aro**, **bareun pyeoneureo**, **oen pyeoneureo**.

The meanings of the particle are as follows:

(1) Manner
   as

Hoewoneu-ro gaiphaeseoyo.
회원으로 가입했어요.
I signed in as a member.

(2) Function
   as

Hanguk-e haksaeng-euro wasseoyo.
한국에 학생으로 왔어요.
I come to Korea as a student.

(3) State
   is; and

**Jeo sonyeoneun Gim seonsaengui ttal-lo
Busaneseo salgo iseoyo.**
저 소녀는 김 선생의 딸로 부산에서 살고
있어요.
That girl is Mr. Kim's daughter and is living in
Pusan.

(4) Direction
   toward; to

Oenjjok-euro gaseyo.
왼쪽으로 가세요
Go to the left.

(5) Means   **Na-neun yeonpil-lo pyeonji-reul sseoyo.**
with, by   나는 연필로 편지를 써요.
I'm writing this letter with a pencil.
Bihaenggi-ro wasseoyo?
비행기로 왔어요?
Did you come by plane?

The 2-shape particle **eun/neun** has the shape **eun** after consonants, **neun** after vowels. For example: **jip-eun**, **hakgyo-neun**. The tricky thing about this particle is its meaning and use. As a tag translation you can try *as for*: as a tag meaning you can think of it as the TOPIC indicator.

What this particle does is take something and set it aside as a sort of stage-setting, as if to say—at the very beginning of your sentence—"Now this is what we're going to talk about." It is a particle of DE-EMPHASIS. The word or phrase in front of it refers to the least unknown ingredient in your communication—the part you'd be most likely to drop if you were going to send a postcard. For this reason, the phrase with this particle nearly always comes at the very beginning of the sentence. (Sometimes it is preceded by an adverb put out of place at the beginning for a kind of special emphasis.)

In Lesson 5 you learned that the important things in a Korean sentence tend to accumulate toward the END, and the less novel parts of your statement, the things the other person is more likely to know, are put closer to the BEGINNING, where they are easier to drop. You also learned that, depending on the situation, the dispensable part of your news—what the other person probably knows already—may be the subject, the object, the place, the time, or anything EXCEPT THE VERB EXPRESSION.

So, if you want to take out any of the phrases in front of the verb and put them at the beginning in order to lessen the emphasis on them, you can then add the particle **eun/neun** to still further cut down their emphasis. When you do this to the subject or object, the ordinary particles (**i/ga** or **eul/reul**) do not occur.

For any other phrases, you can add the topic particle right after whatever particle would ordinarily be there. Let's take an example: **Geu haksaeng-i jigeum hakgyo-eseo Hangungmal-eul gongbu haeyo.** *That student is now studying Korean at school.* With differences of emphasis, this can be said in any of these ways:

Geu haksaeng-eun jigeum hakgyo-eseo Hangungmal-eul gongbu haeyo.

Jigeum geu haksaeng-i hakgyo eseo Hangungmal-eul gongbu haeyo.

Hakgyo-eseo geu haksaeng-i jigeum Hangungmal-eul gongbu haeyo.

Hangungmal-eul geu haksaeng-i jigeum hakgyo-eseo gongbu haeyo.

But just how do you use this reduction of emphasis? It is used, for one thing, when you are making different statements about two different subjects or objects, de-emphasizing these in order to play up their points of CONTRAST:

Hotel-eun boineunde cheolttoyeok-i an boyeoyo.
호텔은 보이는데 철도역이 안보여요.
The hotel I see. But I can't see the railroad station.

In English we usually stress the emphasis the other way: KIM'S in the army, but ME, I'm in the air force. This is why some people will tell you this Korean particle shows emphasis rather than de-emphasis:

Kim seonsaeng-eun yukgun inde, na-neun gonggun imnida.
김 선생은 육군인데 나는 공군입니다.
Kim is (in) the ARMY. But I'm (in) the AIR FORCE.

When you first mention a subject, you usually use the subject particle. But if you keep on talking about the same thing, you either repeat the subject (in the same or slightly different words) with the topic particle, or you just don't mention it:

Nae chingu-neun Miguk-eseo wasseoyo. (Geu-neun) Miguk saram ieyo. (Geu saram-eun) gunin-euro Hanguk-e waseoyo. (Geu saram-eun) yukgun janggyo eyo. (Geu saram-eun) Seoul-eseo salgo isseoyo.
내 친구는 미국에서 왔어요. 그는 미국 사람이에요. 군인으로 한국에 왔어요. 그는 육군 장교에요. 그는 서울에서 살고 있어요.
My friend came from America. He is an American. He came to Korea as a serviceman. He's an army officer. He's living in Seoul.

The one-shape particle **do** is a kind of opposite; it has the meaning *too, also, indeed, even*. This particle reinforces the emphasis on the

preceding word with reference either to some other part of the sentence
or to something outside the sentence:

**Geu haksaeng-do yojeueum hakgyo-eseo Hangungmal-eul gongbu
hago isseoyo.**
그 학생도 요즈음 학교에서 한국말은 공부하고 있어요.
That student is studying Korean in school now too (as well as someone
else). OR Even that student (to my surprise)....

**Geu haksaeng-i jigeum hakgyo-eseo Hangukmal-do gongbu hago
isseoyo.**
그 학생이 지금 학교에서 한국말도 공부하고 있어요.
That student is now studying Korean at school too (as well as at home
or somewhere else). That student is studying Korean at school now too
(as well as other subjects).

Notice that the English words *too* and *also* are ambiguous in reference
wherever you put them in the sentence, but the Korean particle **do**
always refers to the word preceding it. Notice also that the subject and
object particles are not used when you use **do** (just as they are not with
the topic particle).

Since the particle **do** reinforces the emphasis, we might expect
the phrase with which it occurs to be moved over near the end of the
sentence, and this sometimes happens, but it seems to be unnecessary
since the particle itself lends all the emphasis needed.

Now notice the translation of the following sentences:

Bap-do meokgo ppang-do meogeoyo.
밥도 먹고 빵도 먹어요.
Or:
Bap-do ppang-do da meogeoyo.
밥도 빵도 다 먹어요.
I eat both rice and bread.

Achim-edo ilhago bam-edo ilhaeyo.
아침에도 일하고 밤에도 일해요.
Or:
Achim-edo bam-edo da ilhaeyo.
아침에도 밤에도 다 일해요.
I work both in the mornings and in the evenings.

Yeonpil-do sago pen-do saseoyo.

연필도 사고 펜도 샀어요.

I bought both a pencil and a pen.

Migug-eseodo ogo ilbon-eseodo wasseoyo.

미국에서도 오고 일본에서도 왔어요.

They came from both America and Japan.

Jip-do itgo cha-do iseoyo.

집도 있고 차도 있어요.

Or:

Jip-do cha-do da iseoyo.

집도 차도 다 있어요.

I have both a house and a car.

Gim seonsaeng-do, Ma seonsaeng-do, Jang seonsaeng-do mannasseoyo.

김 선생, 마 선생, 장 선생도 만났어요.

I saw Mr. Kim, and Mr. Ma, and Mr. Chang, all three.

When you have **do** after each of two affirmative phrases, the translation is *both… and…* If there are more than two phrases, the translation comes out *and …, and …, and …, all 3 (or 4, or 5)*.

Now look at some negative sentences:

Achim-edo bam-edo il haji anayo.

아침에도 밤에도 일하지 않아요.

I work neither in the morning nor at night.

Jip-do cha-do eopseoyo.

집도 차도 없어요.

I haven't got either a house or a car.

Kim seonsaeng-do, Ma seonsaeng-do, Chang seonsaeng-do manaji anasseoyo.

김 선생도 마 선생도 장 선생도 만나지 않았어요.

I haven't met neither Mr. Kim, nor Mr. Ma, nor Mr. Chang.

The translation is *neither… nor…* or *not either… or…*.

LESSON 15

Numerals

The Koreans have two sets of numerals; one of these they borrowed from the Chinese. Up to 99, both sets are used—for 100 and above you use only the Chinese set. The numerals above 10 are usually in combinations of the first ten numerals: 11 is 10-1, 12 is 10-2, 20 (in the Chinese system) is 2-10. But there are a number of sound changes involved. Some of the native Korean numerals have two shapes: the shortened shape is used only when the numeral is right in front of the word with which you are counting. For example **hana** means *one* but *one o'clock* is **han si** and *one person* is **han saram**:

MEANING	NATIVE NUMERALS		CHINESE NUMERAL
	(ordinary)	(shortened)	
1	**hana** 하나	**han** 한	**il** 일
2	**dul** 둘	**du** 두	**i** 이
3	**set** 셋	**se** 세	**sam** 삼
4	**net** 넷	**ne** 네	**sa** 사
5	**daseot** 다섯		**o** 오
6	**yeoseot** 여섯		**yuk** 육
7	**ilgop** 일곱		**chil** 칠
8	**yeodeol(p)** 여덟		**pal** 팔
9	**ahop** 아홉		**gu** 구
10	**yeol** 열		**sip** 십
11	**yeol hana** 열하나	**yeol han** 열한	**sip il** 십일
12	**yeol dul** 열둘	**yeol du** 열두	**sip i** 십이

MEANING	NATIVE NUMERALS		CHINESE NUMERAL
	(ordinary)	(shortened)	
13	yeol set 열셋	yeol se 열세	sip sam 십삼
14	yeol net 열넷	yeol ne 열네	sip sa 십사
15	yeol daseot 열다섯		sip o 십오
16	yeol yoeseot 열여섯		sim nyuk 십육
17	yeol ilgop 열일곱		sip chil 십칠
18	yeol yoedeol 열여덟		sip pal 십팔
19	yeol ahop 열아홉		sip ku 십구
20	seumul 스물		isip 이십
21	seumul hana	seumul han 스물하나(한)	isip il 이십일
22	seumul dul	seumul du 스물둘(두)	isip i 이십이
23	seumul (s)set	seumul (s)se 스물셋(세)	isip sam 이십삼
24	seumul net	seumul ne 스물넷(네)	isip sa 이십사
25	seumul	dasot 스물다섯	isip o 이십오
26	seumul	yeoseot 스물여섯	isip yuk (i-sim-nyuk) 이십육
27	seumul ilgop 스물일곱		isip chil 이십칠
28	seumul yeodeol(p) 스물여덟		isip pal 이십팔
29	seumul ahop 스물아홉		isip ku 이십구
30	seoreun 서른		samsip 삼십
40	maheun 마흔		sasip 사십
50	swin 쉰		osip 오십
60	yesun 예순		yuksip 육십
70	ilheun 일흔		chil(s)sip 칠십
80	yeodeun 여든		pal(s)sip 팔십
90	aheun 아흔		gusip 구십
100	—		baek; il baek 백, 일백
200			i baek 이백
300			sam baek 삼백
400			sa baek 사백
500			o baek 오백

MEANING	NATIVE NUMERALS	CHINESE NUMERAL
600		yuk baek 육백
700		chil baek 칠백
800		pal baek 팔백
900		gu baek 구백
1000		cheon; ilcheon 천, 일천
2000		i cheon 이천
3000		sam cheon 삼천
4000		sa cheon 사천
5000		o cheon 오천
6000		yuk cheon 육천
7000		chil cheon 칠천
8000		pal cheon 팔천
9000		gu cheon 구천
10,000		man; il man 만, 일만
20,000		i man 이만
30,000		sam man 삼만
100,000		sim man 십만
1,000,000		baek man 백만

Nouns Ending in -*t*

In Lesson 3, we learned that only the consonants **b**, **d**, **g**, **m**, **n**, **ng**, and **l** occur before a pause or another consonant. But some words have basic forms that end in other sounds, and these have to change before a pause or a consonant. When you hear a noun ending in **t** you are not sure whether the basic form of the noun ends in **d**, **s**, **j**, **ch**, or **t**.

As it happens, nearly all these nouns have basic forms that end in **s**, so we can consider the others as individual exceptions and make a rule: a noun which you hear with a final **t**, has a final **s** when it is linked with a particle beginning with a vowel, or when it is linked with the verb **ieyo** "is." Here are some examples:

MEANING	NOUN	PARTICLE	IEYO
thing	**geot** 것	**geos-i** 것이	**geos ieyo** 것이에요
place	**got** 곳	**gos-i** 곳이	**gos ieyo** 곳이에요
what?	**mueot?** 무엇?	**mueos-i?** 무엇이?	**mueos ieyo?** 무엇이에요?
clothes	**ot** 옷	**os-eun** 옷은	**os ieyo** 옷이에요
three	**set** 셋	**ses-i** 셋이	**ses ieyo** 셋이에요

MEANING	NOUN	PARTICLE	IEYO
four	**net** 넷	**nes-eul** 넷을	**nes ieyo** 넷이에요
five	**daseot** 다섯	**daseos-eul** 다섯을	**daseos ieyo** 다섯이에요
six	**yeoseot** 여섯	**yeoseos-i** 여섯이	**yeoseos ieyo** 여섯이에요

The individual exceptions are regularized by many Koreans so that you may hear both forms:

flower	**kkot** 꽃	{ **kkoch-i** 꽃이 { **kkos-i**	**kkoch ieyo** 꽃이에요 **kkos ieyo**
how many?	**myeot?** 몇?	{ **myeoch ina?** { 몇이나? { **myeos ina?**	**myeoch ieyo?** 몇이에요? **myeos ieyo?**
daytime	**nat** 낮	**naj-e** 낮에	**nach ieyo** 낮이에요 **naj ieyo**
dry field	**bat** 밭	{ **bat-e** 밭에 { **bas-e**	**bat ieyo** 밭이에요 **bas ieyo**

Counting Things

In English we can say either *two steers* or *two head of cattle*. In the same way, Koreans say either **so dul** = *two cows* or **so du mari** = *two head of cattle*. But expressions like *two* HEAD *of cattle*, *four* SHEETS *of paper*, *a* CONTAINER *of milk*, *three* PIECES *of candy*, *six* ITEMS *of laundry* are much more common in Korean. The words in capital letters can be called CLASSIFIERS—they tell you something about the shape or looks of the thing you're counting. Or sometimes they tell you the unit by which you are measuring the thing: *three* CUPS *of sugar*, *two* TABLESPOONFULS *of sugar*, *one* POUND *of sugar*. Most Korean classifiers are used with the native set of numerals, but a few common ones are used with the Chinese set. Here are some useful classifiers:

USED WITH KOREAN NUMERALS

si	시	o'clock
sigan	시간	hours
*dal	달	months
sal	살	years old
saram	사람	people
bun	분	honored people
gwon	권	bound volumes
mari	마리	animals, fish
beon	번	times
*jang	장	flat objects, newspapers
*jan	잔	cupfuls
chae	채	buildings
dae	대	vehicles, machines
gae	개	items, units, objects

The starred (*) items count *three* and *four* with the special shapes **seok** and **neok** instead of **se** and **ne**:

seok dal 석 달 *three months*   **neok jang** 넉 장 *four flat objects*

USED WITH CHINESE NUMERALS

bun	분	minutes
(n)yeon	년, 연	years
cheung	층	floor (of buildings)
(l)i, (n)i	리	miles, Li
won	원	won (currency)

Notice that **i bun** means *two minutes* but **du bun** means *two honored persons*.

When you are using a noun, a particle and a number expression (a numeral plus a classifier, or a numeral all by itself), there are three possible ways to phrase your sentence, and all are common.

Chaek du gwon isseoyo.   책 두 권 있어요.
Chaek-i dul isseoyo.   책이 둘 있어요.

These all mean *I have two books*. You can say the same thing with a classifier:

Du gwon-ui chaek-i isseoyo. Chaek du gwon-i isseoyo. Chaek-i du gwon isseoyo.

Here are some examples of number expressions in sentences:

Sinmun-eul du jang sasseoyo.
신문을 두 장 샀어요.
I bought two newspapers.

Achim-mada sinmun-eul myeot jang-ina saseyo?
아침마다 신문을 몇 장이나 사세요?
How many newspapers do you buy each morning?

Jadongcha han dae-man isseoyo.

자동차 한 대만 있어요.

We have only one automobile.

Han pun-do eopseoyo.

한 푼도 없어요.

I haven't a cent.

Gyeongchal se myeong-eul bwasseoyo.

경찰 세 명을 봤어요.

I saw three policemen.

I chaek-eul du beon ilgeosseoyo.

이 책을 두 번 읽었어요.

I read this book twice.

Geu yeongwha-reul se beon bwasseoyo.

그 영화를 세 번 봤어요.

I saw that movie three times.

Jeomwon-ege i cheon won jueosseoyo.

점원에게 이천원 주었어요.

I gave the clerk 2000 won.

I bilding myeot cheung-ina isseoyo?

이 빌딩 몇 층이나 있어요?

How many stories does this building have?

Ot-eun i cheung-eseo parayo.

옷은 이층에서 팔아요.

They sell clothes on the second floor.

Hanguk-e onji beolsseo sam nyeon jjae eyo.

한국에 온 지 벌써 삼년째에요.

I am (= have been) in Korea already three years (long).

Il nyeon dwi-e Miguk-euro doragayo.
일년 뒤에 미국으로 돌아가요.
I go back (return) to America after a year.

I nyeon jeon-e Busan-eseo salgo isseosseoyo.
이년 전에 부산에서 살고 있었어요.
Two years ago (before) I was living in Pusan.

Ttal-i myeot sal ieyo?
딸이 몇 살이에요?
How old is your daughter?

Yeol yeodeol sal ieyo.
열여덟 살이에요.
She's 18.

Jeoneun maheun sal ieyo. An(h)ae-neun seoreun ahop sal ieyo.
저는 마흔 살이에요. 아내는 서른 아홉 살이에요.
I'm 40. My wife is 39.

Telling Time

To say what time it is, you use the Korean numerals followed by **si** = *o'clock*:

| **han si** | one o'clock | 한 시 |
| **du si** | two o'clock | 두 시 |

To say *half-past* you add the word **pan** = *and a half* at the end of the expression:

| **du si ban** | 2:30 | 두 시 반 |

To say *and so-many minutes* you use the Chinese numerals and the noun **bun** = *minutes*:

| **se si sip o bun** | 3:15 | 세 시 십오 분 |

If you want to specify a.m. and p.m. you put the words **ojeon** = *before noon* and **ohu** = *afternoon* in front of the time expression:

| **ojeon ahop si ban** | 9:30 a.m. | 오전 아홉 시 반 |
| **ohu ne si sasip bun** | 4:40 p.m. | 오후 네 시 사십 분 |

To say *so-and-so-many* HOURS you use the Korean numerals and the noun **sigan** = *hour*:

Yeol sigan geollyeoyo.	It takes ten hours.	열 시간 걸려요.
Du sigan geollyeoyo.	We have two hours.	두 시간 걸려요.

Here are some examples of time expressions in sentences:

Myeot si eyo?
몇 시에요?
What time is it?

Han si eyo.
한시에요.
It's one o'clock.

Han si ban ieyo.
한 시 반이에요.
It's 1:30.

Du si sipbun ieyo.
두 시 십 분이에요.
It's 2:10.

Daseot si osip bun ieyo.
다섯 시 오십 분이에요.
It's 5:50.

Ohu ne si sibo bun ieyo.
오후 네 시 십오 분이에요.
It's 4:15 p.m.

Ojeon ahop si ban-e sijak haeyo.
오전 아홉 시 반에 시작해요.
We begin at 9:30 a.m.

Achim yeodeol si-buteo bam yeol si-kkaji bappayo.
아침 여덟 시부터 밤 열 시까지 바빠요.
I'm busy from 8 in the morning till 10 at night.

LESSON 19

What Day Is It?

Counting days is somewhat irregular. Up to 20, the following system is most common, both for counting the days and for giving the day of the month.

How many days?	**Myeochil?**	몇 일?
What day of the month?	**Museun yoil?**	무슨 요일?
1(st)	**haru**	하루
2(nd)	**iteul**	이틀
3(rd)	**saheul**	사흘
4(th)	**naheul**	나흘
5(th)	**dassae**	닷새
6(th)	**yeossae**	엿새
7(th)	**ire**	이레
8(th)	**yeodeure**	여드레
9(th)	**aheure**	아흐레
10(th)	**yeol heul**	열흘
11(th)	**yeol haru**	열하루
12(th)	**yeol iteul**	열이틀
13(th)	**yeol saheul**	열사흘
14(th)	**yeol naheul**	열나흘
15(th)	**yeol dassae**	열닷새
16(th)	**yeol yeossae**	열엿새
17(th)	**yeol ire**	열이레
18(th)	**yeol yeodeure**	열여드레
19(th)	**yeol aheure**	열아흐레
20(th)	**seumu nal**	스무날

But alongside this system, there is also a Chinese system using the classifier **il** = *day* and the regular Chinese numerals: **il il, i il, sam il, sa il, o il**, etc.

Below 20, this is used only for dates, and is more formal than the other way of saying the days: **yuk il** *the 6th day of the month*.

Above 20, this system is the only one used: **i sip il il** = *21 days* OR *the 21st day of the month*; **i sip i il** = *22 days* OR *the 22nd day of the month*; **sam sip sam il** = *33 days*.

The names of the days of the week are as follows:

What day of the week?	**Museun yoil ieyo?** 무슨 요일 이에요?
Monday	**Wol yoil (wo ryo il)** 월요일
Tuesday	**Hwa yoil** 화요일
Wednesday	**Su yoil** 수요일
Thursday	**Mok yoil (Mo gyoil)** 목요일
Friday	**Geum yoil** 금요일
Saturday	**To yoil** 토요일
Sunday	**Il yoil (iryoil)** 일요일

Weeks are counted with either the Korean or the Chinese numerals and for a classifier you can use either **juil** or **jugan**—both mean *week*:

How many weeks?	**Myeot jugan?** 몇 주간?
one week	**han ju, il juil, han jugan, il jugan** 한 주, 일주일, 한 주간, 일주간

two weeks

du ju, i juil, du jugan, i jugan
두 주, 이주일, 두 주간, 이주간

three weeks

se ju, sam juil, se jugan, sam jugan
세 주, 삼주일, 세 주간, 삼주간

Months and Years

Months are COUNTED with the classifier **dal** and the Korean numerals: **Myeot dal, han dal, du dal, seok dal, neok dal, daseot dal** = *how many, 1, 2, 3, 4, 5 months*; or with the classifier **kae-weol** and the Chinese numerals: **il gaewol, i gaewol, sam gaewol, sa gaewol, o gaewol.**

Months are NAMED with combinations of the Chinese numerals and **-wol** = *month*, but there are a few irregularities, starred in the list below.

Notice that January has two names:

January	**Il wol**	(sounds like **i rweol**) 일월
	Jongwol	정월
February	**I wol**	이월
March	**Sam wol**	삼월
April	**Sa wol**	사월
May	**O wol**	오월
June	***Yu wol**	유월
July	**Chil wol**	(sounds like **chi rweol**) 칠월
August	**Pal wol**	(sounds like **pa rweol**) 팔월
September	**Gu wol**	구월
October	***Si wol**	시월
November	**Sip il wol**	(sounds like **si bi rweol**) 십일월
December	**Sip i wol**	(sounds like **si bi weol**) 십이월

The seasons are **bom** = *spring*, **yeoreum** = *summer*, **gaeul** = *autumn*, and **gyeoul** = *winter*.

Years are counted or named by using the Chinese numerals and the classifier **nyeon**, and there are a few sound changes: **il nyeon, i nyeon, sam nyeon, sa nyeon, o nyeon, yuk nyeon (yungnyeon), chil nyeon, pal nyeon, gu nyeon, sip nyeon (simnyeon).**

Note also **baek nyeon** = *100 years*, **cheon nyeon** = *1000 years*.

Dates are given like this: **I cheon chil nyeon, Sip i wol sip o il**. *15 December 2007*. If you want to add the day of the week and the time:

Icheon chil nyeon il wol ku il to yoil ohu sesi sibo bun. *3:15 p.m., Saturday, 9 January 2007.*

Negative Sentences

You have learned to say *no* with **ani** or **ani o**. To make a complete negative sentence, you can use an abbreviated form of this word (**an**) in front of the verb:

Sinmun-eul an sasseoyo.
신문을 안 샀어요.
I didn't buy a newspaper.

Gim seonsaeng-i an wayo.
김 선생이 안 와요.
Mr. Kim isn't coming.

Geu yeonghwa ajik an bwasseoyo.
그 영화 아직 안 봤어요.
I didn't see that movie yet.

But you *do not* use **an** with **isseoyo**: there is a special verb **eopseoyo** = *does not exist*. You can make a stronger negative by using **mot** = *not at all; not possibly; can't* instead of **an**:

Sinmun-eul mot sasseoyo.
신문을 못 샀어요.
I couldn't buy a newspaper.

Gim seonsaeng-i mot wayo.
김 선생이 못 와요.
Mr. Kim can't come; Mr. Kim isn't coming at all.

Juin-eul mot bwasseoyo.

주인을 못 봤어요.

I couldn't see the owner

Except for very short sentences, Koreans prefer to say their negatives in a more complicated way. They change the verb to a special form we'll call the **-ji** form and then add some form of either **an haeyo** = *doesn't do* or **mot haeyo** = *can't possibly do*.

Bumonim-kke jeonhwa-reul an haesseoyo.

부모님께 전화를 안 했어요

I didn't call to my parents.

Bumonim-kke jeonhwa-reul mot haesseoyo.

부모님께 전화를 못했어요.

I couldn't call to my parents.

Yori-reul jal an haeyo.

요리를 잘 안해요.

Usually, I don't cook.

Yori-reul jal mot haeyo.

요리를 잘 못해요.

I can't cook well.

Sukje-reul da an haesseoyo.

숙제를 다 안 했어요.

I didn't do all of my homework.

Sukje-reul da mot haesseoyo.

숙제를 다 못 했어요.

I couldn't do all of my homework

A further complication: Koreans often substitute the verb **anayo** for **an haeyo**. (This **anayo** was originally just a contraction of **an haeyo**.)

Sinmun-eul saji anasseoyo.
신문을 사지 않았어요.
I didn't buy a newspaper.

Beoseu-ga oji anayo.
버스가 오지 않아요.
The bus is not coming.

Geu-ga jeonhwa reul an haeyo.
그가 전화를 안 해요.
He didn't call me.

Here are some examples of negative sentences:

Na-neun hakgyo-eseo gongbu haji anayo.
나는 학교에서 공부하지 않아요.
I don't study in school.

Na-neun don i eopseoyo geu rae seo, geuk jang-e gaji mot haeyo.
나는 돈이 없어요. 그래서 극장에 가지 못해요.
I haven't any money; so I can't go to the theatre.

Geu yeonghwa-reul mot bwasseoyo.
그 영화를 못 봤어요.
I couldn't see that movie.

Gage-e gatjiman, amugeot-do saji mot haeseoyo.
가게에 갔지만 아무것도 사지 않았어요.
I went to the store. But I couldn't buy anything.

Geogi-seo gudu palji anayo?
거기서 구두 팔지 않아요?
Don't they sell shoes there?

Gudu an parayo.
구두 안 팔아요.
They don't sell them at all.

Geu du haksaeng-eun yeongeo-reul jal mot haeyo.

그 두 학생은 영어를 잘 못해요.

Those two students couldn't (didn't) speak in English well.

Na-neun Hangungmal-eul jal mot haeyo.

나는 한국말을 잘 못해요.

I can't speak Korean well.

You will learn to make the **-ji** forms for new verbs in Lesson 23.

The negative of an equational sentence like $A = B$ is a bit different:

English formula	Korean formula	
$A = B$	} A **ga**, B **eyo**	A가 B에요.
A is B		

Examples:

Joe-neun moksa imnida.

저는 목사입니다.

I'm a preacher.

Gimssi-neun seonsaengnim imnida.

김씨는 선생님입니다.

Mr. Kim is a teacher.

English formula	Korean formula	
$A \neq B$	A-**neun**, B-**ga anieyo**	A는 B가 아니에요.
A is not B		

Jeo-neun moksa-ga animnida.

저는 목사가 아닙니다.

I'm not a preacher.

Gimssie-neun seonsaengnim-i anieyo.

김씨는 선생님이 아니에요.

Mr. Kim is not a teacher.

Notice that the affirmative sentence attaches the verb **ieyo** directly to the noun (B) but in the negative sentence the word **ani** is attached to the copula and the noun (B) is followed by the subject particle. The noun A is also followed by the subject particle. (It is the bigger subject of the whole expression B-**ga anieyo**.) But this can be changed to the topic particle in order to emphasize the *not*.

Where Things Are

To locate objects in English you usually need only a preposition (*in, at, on, under, behind*), but sometimes you use a prepositional phrase which includes a noun (*in front of, on top of, at the side of*). This is the usual Korean way of doing it. Here are some of these "place words" which are nouns in Korean. To locate a thing or an event, you use the particle **e** = *at, in*, etc. or **(e)seo** = *happens at* after one of these words:

an	inside (something spacious)	안
sok	inside (something small or rather full)	속
bak	outside	밖
wi	(on) top of, above	위
arae	below, underneath	아래
mit	(at the) bottom of	밑
ap	front	앞
dwi	behind	뒤
yeop	beside	옆
oenjjok	left side of	왼쪽
oreunjjok	right side of	오른쪽
geonneopyeon	across from	건너편
daeum	next (to)	다음
sai	between	사이

Here are some examples:

Jumeoni sok-e mueot-i isseoyo?
주머니 속에 무엇이 있어요?
What do you have in your pocket?

Gim seonsaeng yeop-e nug-a anjayo?
김 선생옆에 누가 앉아요?
Who sits next to Mr. Kim?

Gyohoe yeop-e gongwon-i isseoyo.
교회 옆에 공원이 있어요.
There's a park next to the church.

Changmun bak-euro namu-ga boyeoyo.
창문 밖으로 나무가 보여요.
Outside the window a tree can be seen.

Namu mit-e gae han mari-ga nuwo isseoyo.
나무 밑에 개 한 마리가 누워 있어요.
A dog is lying at the foot of the tree.

Namu wi-e jip han chae-ga isseoyo.
나무 위에 집 한 채가 있어요.
There is a house on top of the tree.

Geu jip an-e sae deul-i salgo isseoyo.
그 집 안에 새들이 살고 있어요.
There are birds living in that house.

Hakgyo oreunjjok-e gil-i isseoyo.
학교 오른쪽에 길이 있어요.
There's a road on the right of the school.

Yeonpil-eul eodi-da dwojji?
연필을 어디다 뒀지?
Where did I put my pencil?

Gabang sok-e dueonna?
가방 속에 두었나?
Did I put it in my briefcase?

Jumeoni sok-e dueonna?
주머니 속에 두었나?
Did I put it in my pocket?

Botong chaeksang wi-e noayo.
보통 책상 위에 놓아요.
Usually I put it on the desk.

Chaeksang arae-(e) eopseoyo?
책상 아래(에) 없어요?
Isn't it under the desk?

Maru wi-e eopseoyo?
마루 위에 없어요?
Isn't it on the floor?

Chaek sai-e isseoyo?
책 사이에 있어요?
Is it between those two books?

Ne, majayo. Chaek sai-e inneyo.
네 맞아요. 책 사이에 있네요.
You're right. It's between this book and that one

Je-ga yeonpil-eul chaek sai-e dueonneyo.
제가 연필을 책 사이에 두었네요.
I put my pencil between that book and this one.

LESSON 23

Verbs and Adjectives

The nucleus of a Korean sentence is the verb expression at the end. A verb in Korean is a word which means either *something happens, someone* DOES *something* or *something* IS *a certain way*.

Most English adjectives correspond to verbs in Korean: **keoyo** = *is big*, **jeogeoyo** = *is little*, **manayo** = *is much, are many*, **ippeoyo** = *is cute* etc. Notice that these Korean words do not mean *big, little, much, cute* but IS *big*, IS *little*, IS *much*, IS *cute*.

Later you will learn how to put such verbs in front of nouns to modify them—in Korean instead of saying *a big house* you have to say the equivalent of *a house which is big*.

Now there are a few English adjectives which correspond to Korean nouns: **sae** = *new*, **on** = *whole, entire*. These can modify a following noun just by being in front of it: **sae moja** = *new hat*, **on segye** = *whole world*. But most English adjectives correspond to Korean verbs.

Each Korean verb appears in a great many different forms—as many as 500. Some of these forms are fairly rare, but many are common. In this book, you will learn a few of the most useful forms and find out a little about the structure of verb forms in general, so that you will be better prepared to cope with the bewildering number of forms you hear.

Each verb form consists of a BASE and an ENDING. Sometimes the ending can be divided into several parts, but we will talk about each ending as a unit. There are two things to learn about each verb base: (1) how it is used, what it means; (2) how its shape changes when you add the various endings. And there are two things to learn about each ending: (A) how it is used, what it means; (B) how its shape changes when you attach it to the various kinds of bases.

Fortunately the shape changes are rather systematic, and if you learn a few typical verbs you can make up forms for new verbs by analogy.

The most complicated rules are for INFINITIVE or **-eo** ending. Since this is the form which occurs with the particle **yo** in the polite style, it is perhaps best just to memorize the verb from this form to start with and find one other form where the base of the verb appears in its basic form.

Below you will find a list of typical verb bases, showing (1) the polite present form (**-eo yo, -a yo, -e yo**, with some irregularities); (2) the polite past form (**-eosseoyo** or **-asseoyo** with some irregularities); (3) the polite present negative (**-ji anayo**). To make the negative past you replace **anayo** with **anasseoyo**:

An jabasseoyo.   **Jabji anasseoyo.**
안 잡았어요.   잡지 안았어요.
did not catch.   didn't catch.

Finally there is given the basic shape of the BASE, from which the various forms are predictable. There are two general classes of bases: CONSONANT and VOWEL. The basic shape of consonant bases is found when you remove the **-eoyo** ending; the basic shape of vowel verbs appears when you take away the **-ji** ending.

1. CONSONANT BASES

BASE	MEANING	DOES; IS	DID; WAS	DOESN'T; ISN'T
jab- 잡	catches	**jabayo** 잡아요	**jabasseoyo** 잡았어요	**jabji anayo** 잡지않아요
nop- 높	is high	**nopayo** 높아요	**nopasseoyo** 높았어요	**nopji anayo** 높지않아요
eops- 없	is non-existent	**eopseoyo** 없어요	**eopseosseoyo** 없었어요	–
dad 닫	closes	**dadayo** 닫아요	**dadasseoyo** 닫았어요	**dajji anayo** 닫지 않아요
kat- 같	is like	**gatayo** 같아요	**gatasseoyo** 같았어요	**gajji anayo** 같지 않아요

BASE	MEANING	DOES; IS	DID; WAS	DOESN'T; ISN'T
us- 웃	laughs	**useoyo** 웃어요	**useosseoyo** 웃었어요	**ujji anayo** 웃지 않아요
iss- 있	exists	**isseoyo** 있어요	**iseosseoyo** 있었어요	–
chaj- 찾	finds	**chajayo** 찾아요	**chajasseoyo** 찾았어요	**chajji anayo** 찾지 않아요
ssijj- 씻	washes	**ssiseoyo** 씻어요	**ssiseosseoyo** 씻었어요	**ssijji anayo** 씻지 않아요
ilg- 읽	reads	**ilgeoyo** 읽어요	**il geosseoyo** 읽었어요	**ilgji anayo** 읽지 않아요
ilh- 잃	loses	**ireoyo** 잃어요	**ireosseoyo** 잃었어요	**ilchi anayo** 잃지 않아요
halt- 핥	licks	**haltayo** 핥아요	**haltaseoyo** 핥았어요	**haljji anayo** 핥지 않아요
balb- 밟	steps on	**balbayo** 밟아요	**balbasseoyo** 밟았어요	**baljji anayo** 밟지 않아요
eulp- 읊	chants	**eulpeoyo** 읊어요	**eulpeosseoyo** 읊었어요	**eupji anayo** 읊지 않아요
noh- 놓	puts	**noayo** 놓아요	**noasseoyo** 놓았어요	**nochi anayo** 놓지 않아요
meog- 먹	eats	**meogeoyo** 먹어요	**meogeosseoyo** 먹었어요	**meokji anayo** 먹지 않아요
kkakk- 깎	cuts	**kkakkayo** 깎아요	**kkakkasseoyo** 깎았어요	**kkakji anayo** 깎지 않아요

BASE	MEANING	DOES; IS	DID; WAS	DOESN'T; ISN'T
gam- 감	shampoos	**gamayo** 감아요	**gamasseoyo** 감았어요	**gamjji anayo** 감지 않아요
jeom- 젊	is young	**jeolmeoyo** 젊어요	**jeolmeosseoyo** 젊었어요	**jeomjji anayo** 젊지 않아요
sin- 신	wears on feet	**sineoyo** 신어요	**sineosseoyo** 신었어요	**sinjji anayo** 신지 않아요
anj- 앉	sits	**anjayo** 앉아요	**anjasseoyo** 앉았어요	**anjji anayo** 앉지 않아요
bureo- 부러	breaks	**bureo-jeoyo** 부러져요	**bureojyeosseoyo** 부러졌어요	**bureojiji anayo** 부러지지 않아요

II. VOWEL BASES

BASE	MEANING	DOES; IS	DID; WAS	DOESN'T; ISN'T
(i)-	is, equals	**ieyo** 이에요	**ieosseoyo** 이었어요	–
		-eyo 에요	**yeosseoyo** 였어요	–
swi- 쉬	rests	**swieoyo** 쉬어요	**swieosseoyo** 쉬었어요	**swiji anayo** 쉬지않아요
gidari- 기다리	waits	**gidaryeoyo** 기다려요	**gidaryeosseoyo** 기다렸어요	**gidariji anayo** 기다리지 않아요
se- 세	counts	**seyo** 세요	**seeosseoyo** 세었어요	**seji anayo** 세지 않아요
dwe- 되	becomes	**dweyo** 되요	**dwesseoyo** 됐어요	**dweji anayo** 되지 않아요

BASE	MEANING	DOES; IS	DID; WAS	DOESN'T; ISN'T
nae-	pays	**naeyo**	**naessoeyo**	**naeji anayo**
내		내요	냈어요	내지 않아요
sseu-	writes	**sseoyo**	**sseosseoyo**	**sseuji anayo**
쓰		써요	썼어요	쓰지 않아요
ga-	goes	**gayo**	**gasseoyo**	**gaji anayo**
가		가요	갔어요	가지 않아요
ju-	gives	**jwoyo**	**jueosseoyo**	**juji anayo**
주		줘요	주었어요	주지 않아요
bo-	sees, reads	**bwayo**	**bwasseoyo**	**boji anayo**
보		봐요	봤어요	보지 않아요

(VOWEL BASES WITH IRREGULAR FORMS)

BASE	MEANING	DOES; IS	DID; WAS	DOESN'T; ISN'T
ha-	does	**haeyo**	**haesseoyo**	**haji anayo**
하		해요	했어요	하지 않아요
bureu-	calls	**bulleoyo**	**bulleosseoyo**	**bureuji anayo**
부르		불러요	불렀어요	부르지 않아요
pureu-	is blue, green	**pureureoyo**	**pureureo-sseoyo**	**pureuji anayo**
푸르		푸르러요	푸르렀어요	푸르지 않아요

NOTE: The **-ji** forms for **isseoyo**, **eopseoyo**, and **ieyo** are **itji**, **eopji**, and **iji**. They are not used in the negative construction.

Most of the other verbs you have met will fit into one of the above categories. For example, **wayo** = *comes* works just like **bwayo** = *sees*:

BASE	MEANING	DOES; IS	DID; WAS	DOESN'T; ISN'T
o-	comes	**wayo**	**wasseoyo**	**oji anayo**
오		와요	왔어요	오지 않아요

Ippeoyo = *is cute* and **keoyo** = *is big* are like **sseoyo** = *writes*:

BASE	MEANING	DOES; IS	DID; WAS	DOESN'T; ISN'T
ippeu- 이쁘	is cute	**ippeoyo** 이뻐요	**ippeosseoyo** 이뻤어요	**ippeuji anayo** 이쁘지 않아요
keu- 크	is big	**keoyo** 커요	**keosseoyo** 컸어요	**keuji anayo** 크지 않아요

jeogeoyo = *is small* works like **meogeoyo** = *eats*. **Manayo** = *is much, are many* and **anayo** = *does not, is not* have forms like those of **kkeuneoyo** = *cuts*; **badayo** = *gets* has forms like those of **dadeoyo** = *closes*. **Mollayo** = *does not know* and **mallayo** = *gets dry* work like **bulleoyo** = *calls*:

BASE	MEANING	DOES; IS	DID; WAS	DOESN'T; ISN'T
mareu- 마르	gets dry		**mallasseoyo** 말랐어요	**mareuji anasseoyo** 마르지 않았어요

Here are a few examples of these verbs in sentences.

Geu san-i nopayo.
그 산이 높아요.
That mountain is tall.

Wae mun-eul dajji anasseoyo?
왜 문을 닫지 않았어요?
Why didn't you close the door?

Geu sonyeon-i nae chingu gajji anayo.
그 소년이 내 친구 같지 않아요.
That boy is not like my friend.

Eodi-eseo geu don-eul chajasseoyo?
어디에서 그 돈을 찾았어요?
Where did you find the money?

Agi-ga wae ujji anayo?
아기가 왜 웃지 않아요?
Why isn't the baby laughing?

Moja-reul ireo beoryeosseoyo.
모자를 잃어버렸어요.
I lost my hat.

Jakeseul rireobeoriji anaseoyo.
자켓을 잃어버리지 않았어요.
I didn't lose my jacket.

Gabang-eul teibeul wie nochi anasseoyo.
가방을 테이블 위에 놓지 않았어요.
I didn't put my briefcase on the table.

Geu-neun gogi-reul meokji anayo.
그는 고기를 먹지 않아요.
He doesn't eat meat (at all).

Neo-ege don-eul juji anatta.
너에게 돈을 주지 않았다.
I didn't give you any money.

Don-i eopseoseo gyesan haji mot haeyo.
돈이 없어서 계산하지 못해요.
I haven't any money; so, I can't pay (you).

Relatives

The Korean terms for relatives can be divided into two groups: those for which some of the words differ according to the sex of the person related (whether we're talking about a man's brother or a woman's brother), and those for which the words are the same regardless of the sex of the person related. In the lists some words are given in capital letters; these are HONORIFIC—they are used about someone else's relatives when you want to show special politeness, or they are used in addressing older relatives of your own:

1. RELATIVE	MAN'S	WOMAN'S
older brother	**HYEONG (NIM)** 형	**oppa, ORABEONIM** 오빠, 오라버님
older sister	**nuna, NUNIM** 누나, 누님	**eonni, HYEONGNIM*** 언니, 형님
younger brother	**dongsaeng, au** 동생, 아우	**namdongsaeng** 남동생
younger sister	**yeodongsaeng** 여동생	**dongsaeng** 동생
brothers	**hyeongje** 형제	**oppa wa nam-dongsaeng** 오빠와 남동생
sisters	**jamae** 자매	**jamae** 자매
spouse	**an(h)ae, buin** 아내, 부인	**nampyeon** 남편

* **Hyeongnim** is used by a married woman to refer to her sister-in-law (married to her husband's older brother).

RELATIVE	MAN'S	WOMAN'S
father-in-law	**jangin** 장인	**siabeoji, SIABEONIM** 시아버지, 시아버님
mother-in-law	**jangmo** 장모	**sieomeoni, SIEOMEONIM** 시어머니, 시어머님

2. RELATIVE	ANYBODY'S
grandfather	**harabeoji, HARABEONIM** 할아버지, 할아버님
grandmother	**halmeoni, HALMEONIM** 할머니, 할머님
parents	**bumo, BUMONIM** 부모, 부모님
father	**abeoji, ABEONIM** 아버지, 아버님
mother	**eomeoni, EOMEONIM** 어머니, 어머님
children	**ai(deul), ae (deul)** 아이들, 애들
son	**adeul, ADEUNIM** 아들, 아드님
daughter	**ttal, TTANIM** 딸, 따님
grandchildren	**sonju, sonjuttal** 손주, 손주딸
grandson	**sonja** 손자
granddaughter	**sonnyeo** 손녀
son-in-law	**sawi** 사위
daughter-in-law	**myeoneuri** 며느리
fiance(e)	**yakhonja** 약혼자
cousin	**sachon** 사촌

RELATIVE	ANYBODY'S
uncle	**ajeossi, samchon, keun abeoji, jageun abeoji**
	아저씨, 삼촌, 큰아버지, 작은아버지
aunt	**ajumeoni, imo, gomo**
	아주머니, 이모, 고모
nephew or niece	**joka**
	조카
niece	**yeoja joka**
	여자 조카
nephew	**namja joka**
	남자 조카
family	**gajok, jip, daek**
	가족, 집, 댁
members of family	**sikku**
	식구

NOTE: The words for *grandfather* and *grandmother* are also used to mean *old man* and *old woman*. The words for *uncle* and *aunt* are used to mean *(older) man, (older) lady* especially in expressions by and to children like: *The man who lives next door to us; Say hello to the lady, dear.*

Here are some examples of these words in sentences.

Uri gajok-eun daegajok ieyo. Sikku-ga manayo.
우리 가족은 대가족이에요. 식구가 많아요.
My (our) family's large; there are a lot of us.

Myeot bun iseoyo?
몇 분이세요?
How many (honored persons) are you?

Yeol han sikku eyo. Na-hago, anae, ttal dul, adeul set-i isseoyo.
일곱 식구에요. 나하고, 아내, 딸 둘 아들 셋이있어요.
There are seven. My wife and I, two daughters. and three sons.

Abeomnim, eomeonim-i jeohi-hago saseyo.
아버님, 어머님이 저희하고 사세요.
Father and Mother are living with us.

Bumonim kkaji modu ahop saram ieyo.
부모님까지 모두 아홉 사람이에요.
Together with my parents that is nine.

Ajik du saram deo itji anayo?
아직 두 사람 더 있지 않아요?
Aren't there still two people (more)?

Nugu nugu eyo?
누구 누구에요?
Who (and who) are they?

Goyangi han mari hago gae han mari eyo.
고양이 한 마리하고 개 한 마리에요.
They are a cat and a dog.

Jageun abeoji-ga ttal-ege goyangi-reul jusyeosseoyo.
작은아버지가 딸에게 고양이를 주셨어요.
Uncle gave the cat to my daughter.

Yeopjip harabeoji-kkeseo gae-reul jusyeosseoyo.
옆집 할아버지께서 개를 주셨어요.
The old man next door gave the dog to our family.

LESSON 25

Honorifics

When you talk about someone who has a relatively high social status—a
government official, a foreign guest, a minister, a teacher—you use some
special forms called HONORIFICS. These forms are also frequently used
of the second person—it's often a way to show I'm talking about YOU
without actually using a pronoun.

You have come across some honorific nouns already:

bun	an honored person 분	
abeonim	honored father (or father of an honored person) 아버님	
daek	honored house or family –댁	
jinji	honored food 진지	

We even find an honorific particle **kke** = *to* or *for* (*an honored
person*)—this is the honorific equivalent of **hante**, **ege**, and **bogo**:

Harabeoji-kke pyeonji-reul sseosseoyo.
할아버지께 편지를 썼어요.
I wrote a letter to Grandfather.

Kkeseo means *from an honored person*:

Moksa nim-kkeseo pyeonji-reul sseusyeoseoyo.
목사님께서 편지를 쓰셨어요.
I received a letter from the pastor.

There are also a few special honorific verbs. For *an honored person eats* instead of **meogeoyo** you use **chapsuseyo** or **chapsueoyo**. For *an honored person stays or is in a place* you use **keseyo** instead of **isseyo**:

Abeonim-i daek-e keseyo?
아버님이 댁에 계세요?
Is your father at home?

But for the meaning *an honored person has something* you use **iseueseyo**, the expected honorific of **iseyo**:

Abeonim-i geu japji-reul gajigo geseyo?
아버님이 그 잡지를 가지고 계세요?
Does your father have that magazine?

The negative of **geseyo** is **an geseyo**:

Jip-e eomeon-i geseyo?
집에 어머니 계세요?
Is your mother at home?

Daek-e an geseyo?
댁에 안 계세요?
Isn't she at home?

Most verbs are made honorific very easily—you just slip a suffix onto the base before you attach the endings. The suffix has the basic shape **-eusi-** after a consonant base, **-si-** after a vowel base. But the final **i** drops when the ending begins with a vowel.

Here are some examples with verbs you have had:

MEANING	ORDINARY		HONORIFIC	
	PRESENT	PAST	PRESENT	PAST
catches	**jabayo**	**jabaseoyo**	**jabeuseyo**	**jabeusyeosseoyo**
	잡아요	잡았어요	잡으세요	잡으셨어요

MEANING	ORDINARY		HONORIFIC	
	PRESENT	PAST	PRESENT	PAST
closes	**dadayo**	**dadasseoyo**	**dadeuseyo**	**dadeusyeo-sseoyo**
	닫아요	닫았어요	닫으세요	닫으셨어요
laughs	**useoyo**	**useosseoyo**	**useuseyo**	**useusyeosseoyo**
	웃어요	웃었어요	웃으세요	웃으셨어요
reads	**ilgeoyo**	**ilgeosseoyo**	**ilgeuseyo**	**ilgeusyeo-sseoyo**
	읽어요	읽었어요	읽으세요	읽으셨어요
puts	**noayo**	**noasseoyo**	**noeuseyo**	**noeusyeo-sseoyo**
	놓아요	놓았어요	놓으세요	놓으셨어요
cuts	**kkakkayo**	**kkakka-sseoyo**	**kkakkeu-seyo**	**kkakkeu-syeosseoyo**
	깎아요	깎았어요	깎으세요	깎으셨어요
sits	**anjayo**	**anjasseoyo**	**anjeuseyo**	**anjeusyeo-sseoyo**
	앉아요	앉았어요	앉으세요	앉으셨어요
rests	**swieoyo**	**swieoseoyo**	**swiseyo**	**swisyeosseoyo**
	쉬어요	쉬었어요	쉬세요	쉬셨어요
pays	**naeyo**	**naeosseoyo**	**naeseyo**	**naesyeosseoyo**
	내요	내었어요	내세요	내셨어요
writes	**sseoyo**	**sseosseoyo**	**sseuseyo**	**sseusyeosseoyo**
	써요	썼어요	쓰세요	쓰셨어요

MEANING	ORDINARY		HONORIFIC	
	PRESENT	PAST	PRESENT	PAST
goes	**gayo** 가요	**gasseoyo** 갔어요	**gaseyo** 가세요	**gasyeosseoyo** 가셨어요
gives	**jwoyo** 줘요	**jueosseoyo** 주었어요	**juseyo** 주세요	**jusyeosseoyo** 주셨어요
sees	**bwayo** 봐요	**bwasseoyo** 봤어요	**boseyo** 보세요	**bosyeosseoyo** 보셨어요
reads	**ilgeoyo** 읽어요	**ilgeosseoyo** 읽었어요	**ilgeoboseyo** 읽어보 세요	**ilgeobo-syeosseoyo** 읽어보셨 어요
does	**haeyo** 해요	**haesseoyo** 했어요	**haseyo** 하세요	**hasyeosseoyo** 하셨어요

For negative honorific statements, you can make either the **-ji** form or the **anayo** honorific; or if you really want to do it up fancy, make both of them honorific: **jusiji anayo, juji aneuseyo, jusiji aneuseyo, juji aneusyeosseoyo, jusiji aneusseoseoyo.**

In addition to the verb **jwoyo** = *gives* there is another verb **deuryeo yo** = *gives to someone honored*. So **juseyo** means *someone honored gives* or *you give me*, **deuryeo yo** means *I give someone honored* or *I give you*, and **deulise yo** means *someone honored gives someone honored* or *you give someone honored*.

When you command someone to do something, it's good to use the honorific form of the verb:

Iri oseyo!
이리 오세요
Come here!

Juseyo!
주세요
Give (it to me)!

Notice how the use of honorifics makes a conversation between YOU and ME quite clear even though we don't use pronouns:

Eodi gaseyo?
어디 가세요?
Where are you going?

Ucheguk-e gayo.
우체국에 가요.
I'm going to the post office.

Eodi danyeooseyo?
어디 다녀오세요?
Where did you come from?

Jip-eseo naon geoeyo.
집에서 나온 거에요.
I came from home.

Jinji japsusyeosseoyo?
진지 잡수셨어요?
Have you eaten?

Ajik an meogeosseoyo.
아직 안 먹었어요.
I haven't eaten yet.

Gim Gildong abeonim iseyo?
김길동 아버님이세요?
Are you Kim Kildong's father?

Aniyo. Gim Haksu abeoji eyo.
아니요. 김학수 아버지에요.
No, I'm Kim Haksu's father.

Mueot-eul haseyo?
무엇을 하세요?
What do you do?

Seonsaengnim ieyo.
선생님이에요.
I'm a teacher.

Yeongeo-reul gareuchyeoyo.
영어를 가르쳐요.
I teach English.

Myeongham-i isseoyo?
명함이 있어요?
Do you have a name card?

Beolsseo deuriji anasseoyo?
벌써 드리지 않았어요?
Didn't I already give it to you?

Gabang-eul eodi-da dueottura?
가방을 어디다 두었더라?
Where did I put the briefcase?

The Word "But"

You have learned the expression **geureochiman** = *but*:

Gage e gaseoyo. Geureochiman gudureul an saseoyo.
가게에 갔어요 그렇지만 구두를 안 샀어요.
I went to the store. But I didn't buy any shoes.

If you want to link two such sentences together more closely, you can change the verb of the first to the **-ji** form and add the particle **man**:

Gage e gajji man, gudu-reul an sasseoyo.
가게에 갔지만 구두를 안 샀어요.
I went to the store, but I didn't buy any shoes.

If the verb is in the past, you have to use the past **-ji** form which ends in **-eojji** or **-ajji** (with some irregularities, just like the polite past **-eosse yo** and **-ase yo**):
Sangjeom-e gaseyo. Geureochiman, gudu-reul an sasseyo. =
Sangjeom-e kajji man gudu-reul an sasseoyo.

Here are some past **-ji** forms:

jabajjiman	잡았지만	caught but
dadajjiman	닫았지만	closed but
useojjiman	웃었지만	laughed but
noajjiman	놓았지만	put but
anjeusyeojjiman	앉으셨지만	someone honored sat but
sseojjiman	썼지만	wrote but

gasyeojjiman	가셨지만	someone honored went but
jueojjiman	주었지만	gave but
bwajjiman	봤지만	saw but
haejiman	했지만	did but
kaji anajjiman	가지 않았지만	didn't go but
oji aneusyeojjiman	오지않으셨지만	someone honored didn't come but

Here are some examples in sentences:

Eoje-neun ilhaejjiman, oneul-eun swieoyo.
어제는 일했지만 오늘은 쉬어요.
Yesterday I worked but today, I am off (I rest).

Sinmun-eul bwajjiman, geu sajin-eun mot bwasseoyo.
신문을 봤지만 그 사진은 못 봤어요.
I read the newspaper, but I didn't see that picture.

Chaek-eun ilgeojjiman, yeonghwa-neun mot bwasseoyo.
책은 읽었지만 영화는 못봤어요.
I read the book, but I didn't get to see the movie.

Yeonghwa-neun mot bwajjiman chaek-eun ilgeosseoyo?
영화는 못 봤지만 책은 읽었어요.
You didn't see the movie, but you read the book?

Jip-i jakjiman yeppeoyo.
집이 작지만 예뻐요.
The house is small but it's cute.

Gae-ga yeppeujiman neomu jijeoyo.
개가 예쁘지만 너무 짖어요.
The dog is cute but he barks a lot.

Na-neun haksaeng ijiman nae chingu-neun anieyo.
나는 학생이지만 내친구는 아니에요.
I'm a student, but my friend isn't.

Gim seonsaeng-eun Hanguk saram ijiman, Ma seonsaeng-eun Jungguk saram ieyo.

김 선생은 한국 사람이지만 마선생은 중국 사람이에요.

Mr. Kim is a Korean, but Mr. Ma is Chinese.

Na-neun Ilbon-eseo wajjiman, Ilbon saram-eun anieyo.

나는 일본에서 왔지만 일본 사람은 아니에요.

I came from Japan, but I'm not Japanese.

Sikku-neun maneunde don-i eopseoyo.

식구는 많은데 돈이 없어요.

I have a big family, but I haven't any money.

Nae-ga neo-ege jun don-eul da sseokkuna.

내가 너에게 준 돈을 다 썼구나.

I gave you money but you spent it all.

NOTE: **Sseoyo** means (1) *writes*, (2) *uses*, (3) *spends*, (4) *wears on head*. Below, **jagi** means *oneself*.

Geuga moja-reul sseojjiman, jagi moja-ga anieosseoyo.

그가 모자를 썼지만 자기 모자가 아니었어요.

He put on a hat but it wasn't his own.

Pen-i eopseojjiman, chingu yeonpil-lo sseosseoyo.

펜이 없었지만 친구 연필로 썼어요.

I didn't have a pen, but I used a friend's pencil.

Yeonpil-lo sseojjiman, gwaen chanayo.

연필로 썼지만 괜찮아요.

You wrote with a pencil, but it doesn't make any difference.

Infinitives and Favors

The infinitive is the form we get when we drop the particle **yo**: **hae** = *do*, **ga** = *go*, **masyeo** = *drink*, **anjeo** = *sit*, **noa** = *put*, **ilgeo** = *read*. But the infinitives of **iseoyo**, **eopseoyo** and **gatayo** are **iseo**, **eopseo** and **gata**. (Some people say **isseoyo** for **iseoyo**, **eopsseoyo** for **eopseoyo**, and **gateyo** for **gatayo**.) And the infinitives of honorific verbs which end in **-(u)seyo** have the ending **-(eu)seo**: **japsuseyo** = *someone honored eats* but **japswo**. There is also a past infinitive with the ending **-eoseo** or **-aseo** (with all the usual irregularities). The basic rule for making the infinitive from the base is this:

Add **-a** if the vowel of the preceding syllable is **o**, otherwise add **-eo**. But the infinitives of vowel bases are a bit more difficult, and the rules depend on which vowel the base ends in; it is probably easiest just to learn the infinitives without worrying how they are made.

The infinitive form is used in a great many ways. It should not be confused with the English form called infinitive—the two have little or nothing in common.

One way you will hear the infinitive form is all by itself at the end of a sentence in the FAMILIAR style. This style is just like the POLITE style you have learned, except that you drop the **yo** at the end (and usually change **-e** to **-eo**):

POLITE
Eodi-seo wasseoyo?
어디서 왔어요?
Where are you from?

FAMILIAR
Eodi-seo wasseo?
어디서 왔어?

Mueot-eul haeyo?
무엇을 해요?
What do you do?

Mwo hae?
뭐 해?

Gongjang-eseo il haeyo?
공장에서 일해요?
Do you work at the factory?

Gongjang-eseo il hae?
공장에서 일해?

Ilgop si-e meogeoyo?
일곱시에 먹어요.
Do you eat at 7?

Ilgop si-e meogeo?
일곱시에 먹어?

Gongbu haji anayo?
공부하지 않아요?
Don't you study?

Gongbu haji ana?
공부하지 않아?

Another way to use the infinitive is in linking two verbs:

dorayo	돌아요	turns
dorawayo	돌아와요	comes back, returns
doragayo	돌아가요	goes back, returns
deureowayo	들어와요	comes in
deureokayo	들어가요	goes in
nawayo	나와요	comes out
nagayo	나가요	goes out
anjayo	앉아요	sits
anja isseoyo	앉아있어요	is seated
nuwoyo	누워요	lies down
nuwo isseoyo	누워있어요	is lying, is prone

With the verbs **jueoyo** = *gives* and **deuryeoyo** = *gives to someone honored*, this is the way to report a favor:

Abeoji kkeseo pyeonji-reul sseo jueosseoyo.
어버지께서 편지를 써 주셨어요.
Father wrote the letter for me (he gave me the favor of writing the letter).

Ajumeoni-ga aideul-hante iyagi-reul hae jusyeosseoyo.

아주머니가 아이들한테 이야기를 해 주셨어요.

The aunt told the children a story.

Adeul-i abeoji-ui gudu-reul dakka deuryeosseoyo.

아들이 아버지의 구두를 닦아 드렸어요.

The boy shined his father's shoes (for him).

The person FOR whom the favor is done is the INDIRECT OBJECT and takes the particle **hante** (or its equivalents **ege** or **bogo**, or its honorific equivalent **kke**).

To ask someone for a favor you can use the infinitive **juseyo** = (*someone honored*, that is YOU) *please give* or the FORMAL style command **jusipsio** = *please give*:

Don-eul juseyo. Doneul jusipsio.

돈을 주세요. 돈을 주십시오.

Please give me some money.

Don-eul naejusipsio.

돈을 내주십시오.

Please (do me the favor of) pay(ing) the money.

Naeil uri jip-e wa jusipsio.

내일 우리 집에 와 주십시오.

Please come to our house tomorrow.

Jom deo japsuseyo.

좀 더 잡수세요.

Please eat a little more.

Iyagi-reul hae juseyo.

이야기를 해주세요.

Tell us a story.

Mannyeonpil-lo sseo juseyo.

만년필로 써 주세요.

Please write with a fountain pen.

Igeot-eul bada jusipsio.

이것을 받아 주십시오.

Please take (accept) this.

Yeogi-e noa juseyo.

여기에 놓아주세요.

Put it here, please.

To make a negative request you use the **-ji** (or **-eusiji**) form followed by the auxiliary verb **maseyo** = *avoid* or its FORMAL style command form **masipsio**:

Yeongeo-ro mal haji maseyo.

영어로 말하지 마세요.

Don't speak English.

Geogi anjji masipsio.

거기 앉지 마십시오.

Don't sit there.

Yeonpil-lo sseuji maseyo.

연필로 쓰지 마세요.

Don't write with a pencil.

I geo saji maseyo.

이거 사지 마세요.

Don't buy this.

Expressing "May" and "Must"

The infinitive plus **do** means *even though*. Sometimes this is similar to the meaning of **-jiman** = *but*.

Don-i eopseodo haengbok haeyo.
돈이 없어도 행복해요.
Even though I have no money I am happy.

Don-i eopjiman, haengbok haeyo.
돈이 없지만 행복해요.
I have no money, but I am happy.

Usually you use a present infinitive in front of **do** even if the meaning is past, because the sentence makes this clear.

Chaek-i eopseodo, hakgyo-e gasseoyo.
책이 없어도 학교에 갔어요.
I went to school even though I didn't have my book.

Geu yeonghwa jaemi eopseosseodo, jip-e doragaji anasseoyo.
그 영화 재미 없었어도 집에 돌아 가지 않았어요.
Even though the movie was no good, I didn't go home.

This construction is used in asking or giving PERMISSION. To say *may I, can I, will you let me, is it OK* to the Korean says something like *even if I do it, is it all right?* or *even though I do it, does it make any difference?* The word for "all right" is **joayo** = *is good* or **gwaen chanayo** = *makes no difference*.

Iljik wado gwaen chanayo?
일찍 와도 괜찮아요?
Is it all right if I come early?

Oneul bangmun haedo joayo?
오늘 방문해도 좋아요?
Can I visit you today?

Naeil jechul haedo gwaen chanayo.
내일 제출해도 괜찮아요.
You can (I can) hand in the report tomorrow.

I bang an-e gyesyeodo joayo.
이 방안에 계셔도 좋아요.
You may stay in this room.

Yeogi anjado gwaen chanayo.
여기 앉아도 괜찮아요.
You can sit here.

To express OBLIGATION, you use the infinitive (or the honorific infinitive) plus **-ya haeyo** which means something like *has to, must, has got to*. The particle **ya** has a meaning something like *only if you do* and the **haeyo** means *(then) it will do*. In other words, *only if you...will it do = you have to....*

Oneul bam iljjik dorawaya haeyo.
오늘 밤 일찍 돌아와야 해.
You have to come back early tonight.

Yeolsimhi gongbu haeya haeyo.
열심히 공부해야 해요.
I have to study hard (or well).

Hakgyo-e gaya haeyo?
학교에 가야 해요?
Do I have to go to school?

Don-eul naeya haeyo?
돈을 내야 해요?
Do I have to pay the money?

Na-neun i chaek-eul ilgeoya haeyo.
나는 이 책을 읽어야 해요.
I've got to read this book.

Yeogi anjaya haeyo?
여기 앉아야 해요?
Do I have to sit here?

Eoje mueot-eul haeya haesseoyo?
어제 무엇을 해야 했어요?
Yesterday what did I have to do?

Sae pen-eul saya haeyo.
새 펜을 사야 해요.
I have to buy a new pen.

Jigeum je-ga mueot-eul haeya haeyo?
지금 제가 무엇을 해야 해요?
What do I have to do now?

To deny obligation—*you don't have to, you need not*—you say something like *it's all right even if you don't*: **-ji anado joa yo** or **-ji anado gwaen chanayo**, **-ji anado dweyo**.

Iljjik doraoji anado gwaen chanayo.
일찍 돌아 오지 않아도 괜찮아요.
You don't have to come back early.

Hakgyo-e angado dweyo.
학교에 안가도 돼요.
You don't have to go to school.

I chaek-eul boji anado gwaen chanayo.

이 책을 보지 않아도 괜찮아요.

I don't have to read this book.

Geogi anjji anado dweyo.

거기 앉지 않아도 돼요.

You don't have to sit there. (It's OK if you don't sit there.)

Sae pen-eul saji anado dweyo.

새 펜을 사지 않아도 돼요.

You don't have to buy a new pen.

Geu chaek-eun jigeum ilji anado dweyo.

그 책은지금 읽지 않아도 돼요.

That book doesn't have to be read now.

**Geu pyeonji-neun jigeum sseuji anado dwejiman i pyeonji-neun
kkok sseoya haeyo.**

그 편지는 지금 쓰지 않아도 되지만 이 편지는꼭 써야 해요.

That letter doesn't have to be written now, but this letter I have to write
for sure (**kkok**).

Helping Verbs

You have learned that the verbs **joayo** = *gives* and **deuryeoyo** = *gives to someone honored* have special meanings following an infinitive: *does the favor of doing, does* FOR *someone.*

Verbs which have special meanings of this sort when used with other verbs are called HELPING VERBS. Most helping verbs are used in combination with the infinitive form, but some are used with other forms.

The verb **bwayo** ordinarily means *looks, sees, reads* but as a helping verb it means *tries doing*—NOT *tries* TO *do* but *tries do*ING, that is, *samples the act to see what it's like*:

Hangungmal-lo pyeonji-reul sseo bwasseoyo.
한국말로 편지를 써 봤어요.
I tried writing a letter in Korean.

Hanguk sinmun-eul ilgeo bwasseoyo.
한국 신문을 읽어 봤어요.
I tried reading a Korean newspaper.

Cheoncheonhi mal hae bwajjiman, geu saram-i ihae haji mot haesseoyo.
천천히 말해 봤지만 그 사람이 이해하지 못했어요.
I tried talking slowly, but he couldn't understand me.

Hanguk eumsik jom deusyeo boseyo.

한국 음식 좀 드셔 보세요.

Try eating a little Korean food.

This exploratory construction **-e wayo** is often used with *going* and *coming*:

Ilbon-e ga bosyeosseoyo?

일본에 가 보셨어요.

Have you been to Japan? (Did you try going to Japan? Did you go to Japan to see how things are there?)

The verb **beoryeoyo** means *throws away, discards*.

As a helping verb it means *does something completely, for good; puts an end to something*.

Yeolsoe-reul ireo beoryeosseoyo.

열쇠를 잃어 버렸어요.

I lost the key.

Uri jipe-gaega isseojjiman, dudal jeon-e jugeo beoryeosseoyo.

우리 집에 개가 있었지만 두 달 전에 죽어 버렸어요.

We had a dog at our house, but it died two months ago.

Don-eul da sseo beoryeosseoyo?

돈을 다 써버렸어요?

Did you spend all the money?

The verb **dueoyo** means *puts away (for a long time), gets out of the way, stores*:

Bon-i wasseoyo. Gyeoul ot-eul eodi-da dwoyo?

봄이 왔어요. 겨울옷을 어디다 둬요?

Spring has come; where do we put the winter clothes?

Gyeoul-i wasseoyo. Wae yeoreum mulgeon-eul chiuji anasseoyo?
겨울이 왔어요. 왜 여름 물건을 치우지 않았어요?
Fall has come. Why haven't you stored the summer things yet?

Uri-neun ot-eul i jang an-e dueosseoyo.
우리는 옷을 이 장 안에 두었어요.
We kept clothes in this closet.

Geu japji-reul doseogwan-e dueosseoyo.
그 잡지를 도서관에 두었어요.
They put those magazines in the library.

As a helping verb, **dueoyo** means *gets something done that has to be done, does something up:*

Eomeoni-ga ot-eul ppara dusyeosseoyo.
어머니가 옷을 빨아 두셨어요.
Mother washed the clothes, got the laundry done.

Geu daeum jip an-eul cheongso hasyeosseoyo.
그 다음 집 안을 청소 하셨어요.
Then, (next) she cleaned (inside) the house.

Geurigo naseo harabeoji-kke pyeonji-reul sseusyeossoyo.
그리고 나서 할아버지께 편지를 쓰셨어요.
After that she wrote grandfather a letter.

The verb **noayo** means *puts aside (for later use), lays something somewhere (with the expectation of using it again later).* As a helping verb it means something like *does for later; gets something done (so that it will be ready for later use):*

Naeil gongbu-reul eojet bam-e hae nwaseoyo.
내일 공부를 어젯밤에 해 놨어요.
I did tomorrow's lesson (studying) last night.

Geum yoil-kkaji i chaek-eul ilgeo noeuseyo.

금요일까지 이 책을 읽어 놓으세요.

Please read this book by Friday.

Myeot si-e eumsik junbi hae noeulkkayo?

몇시에 음식 준비 해 놓을까요?

What time should you get the meal ready?

Sae gongchaek-eul sa noasseoyo.

새 공책을 사 놓았어요.

I bought a new notebook (to use).

Pyo-reul jigeum sa noeulkkayo?

표를 지금 사 놓을까요?

Can we buy the tickets now (in advance)?

The -go Verb Form

A very common verb form is the gerund or **-go** form. This has a number of uses and we can give it the tag translations of *doing* or *does and, is and*. The form is made by adding **-go** to the verb base in much the same way that **-ji** is added.

MEANING	BASE	-JI FORM	-KO FORM
catches	jab-	japji	japgo
is high	nop-	nopji	nopgo
is nonexistent	eops-	eopji	eopgo
closes	dad-	dajji	dakko
is like	gat-	gajji	gakko
laughs	us-	ujji	ukko
exists	iss-	ijji	ikko
finds	chaj-	chajji	chakko
washes	ssich-	ssijji	ssikko
reads	ilg-	iljji	ilkko or ikko
loses	ilh-	ilchi	ilko
licks	halt-	haljji	halkko
steps on	balb-	baljji	balkko
chants	eulp-	euljji	eulkko
puts	noh-	nochi	noko
eats	meok-	meokji	meokko
cuts	kkakk-	kkakji	kkakko
shampoos	gam-	kamjji	kamkko
is young	jeolm-	jeomjji	jeomkko
wears on feet	sin-	sinjji	sinkko

sits	**anj-**	**anjji**	**ankko**
breaks	**bureo-**	**bureoji**	**bureojigo**
equals, is	**(i)-**	**iji, -ji**	**igo, -go**
rests	**swi-**	**swiji**	**swigo**
(honorific)	**-(eu)si**	**-(eu)siji**	**-(eu)sigo**
pays	**nae-**	**naeji**	**naego**
writes	**sseu-**	**sseuji**	**sseugo**
goes	**ga-**	**gaji**	**gago**
gives	**ju-**	**juji**	**jugo**
sees	**bo-**	**boji**	**bogo**
does	**ha-**	**haji**	**hago**

One use of the gerund to mean *doing* is with the auxiliary **isseoyo** *is* or **geseyo** *someone honored is*:

Abeoji-ga mun-eul dakko isseoyo.
아버지가 문을 닫고 있어요.
Father is shutting the door.

Aegi-ga ukko isseosseoyo.
애기가 웃고 있었어요.
The baby was laughing.

Museun chaek-eul ilkko geseyo?
무슨 책을 읽고 계세요?
What book are you reading?

Geu ttae hyuga yeosseoyo.
그 때 휴가였어요.
I was off (resting) that day.

Gongbu-reul hago geseyo?
공부를 하고 계세요?
Are you doing your lesson?

Yeopseo-reul sseugo isseoyo.
엽서를 쓰고 있어요.
I'm writing a postcard.

Notice that some verbs have slightly different meanings in the *is doing* form:

ibeoyo	입어요	puts on (clothes), wears
ipko isseoyo	입고있어요	is wearing
sseoyo	써요	puts on (hat), wears (hat)
sseugo isseoyo	쓰고 있어요	is wearing (hat)
sineoyo	신어요	puts on (shoes, socks), wears (shoes, socks)
sinkko issoeyo	신고있어요	is wearing (shoes, socks)

Geu japji-reul chaja boajjiman, chajji mot haesseoyo.
그 잡지를 찾아 보았지만 찾지 못했어요.
I was LOOKING FOR that magazine, but I couldn't FIND it.

The second use of the gerund is in the meaning *does and (then)* or *is and (also)*:

Ot-eul ipkko, gudu-reul sinkko, moja-reul sseoyo.
옷을 입고, 구두를 신고 모자를 써요.
I put on clothes, shoes, and hat.

Igeot-eun nae moja igo, jeogeot-eun adeul moja eyo.
이것은 내 모자이고 저것은 아들 모자에요
This is my hat and that is my son's.

You could say these ideas in short, abrupt sentences using the connective word **geurigo** = *does and, is and*:

Os-eul ipkko: Geurigo, gudu-reul sineoyo: Geurigo moja-reul sseoyo.
Igeot-eun nae moja eyo. Geurigo, geu geot-eun adeul moja eyo.

To say *did and then; was and (also)* you can use the ordinary gerund, letting the final past form carry the meaning throughout:

Ot-eul ipko, gudu-reul sinkko, moja-reul sseosseoyo.
옷을 입고 ,구두를 신고 모자를 썼어요
I put on my clothes, my shoes and my hat.

Igeot-eun nae moja igo, jeogeot-eun adeul moja yeosseoyo.

이것은 내 모자이고, 저것은 아들 모자였어요.

This was my hat, and, that was my son's.

Or, you can use a special past gerund (**-eokko**, **-akko**, with the usual irregularities of the infinitive **-eo**, **-a** and the past **-eoss-**, **-ass-**):

Ot-eul ibeokko gudu-reul sineokko, moja-reul sseosseoyo. Igeot-eun nae maja yeokko, geu geot-eun adeul moja yeosseoyo.

Wants and Likes

To say *I want to* … or *I would like to* … use the gerund form of the verb
followed by the helping word **sipeoyo** = *is desired*:

Geu yeonghwa bogo sipeoyo.
그 영화 보고 싶어요.
I want to see that movie.

Dambae-reul sago sipeoyo.
담배를 사고 싶어요.
I want to buy some cigarettes.

Dambae-reul pigo sipeoyo.
담배를 피고 싶어요.
I want to smoke (cigarettes).

Jigeum meokko sipeoyo!
지금 먹고 싶어요.
I want to eat right now!

Gidarigo sipji anayo.
기다리고 싶지 않아요.
I don't want to wait.

Iyaegi-reul hae deurigo sipeoyo.
이야기를 해드리고 싶어요.
I want to tell you a story.

Oneul pyo-reul sa noko sipeoyo.
오늘 표를 사놓고 싶어요.
I want to buy the tickets today (in advance).

Gim seonsaeng-hante mal hago sipeoyo.
김 선생한테 말하고 싶어요.
I want to speak to Mr. Kim.

Jip e gago sipeoyo.
집에 가고 싶어요.
I want to go home.

Na-neun Hanguk-e ikko sipeoyo.
나는 한국에 있고 싶어요.
I want to stay in Korea.

Ilbon-e dora gago sipji anayo.
일본에 돌아가고 싶지 않아요.
I don't want to go back to Japan.

But to say someone other than yourself *wants to* you usually use **sipeohaeyo** instead of **sipeoyo**. You can use **sipeohaeyo** to mean *I want to* but it's rather strong like *I'm longing to.*

To say *someone likes something* you use the expression **joahaseyo** (**hae, hana**):

Geu yeonghwa joasseoyo?
그 영화 좋았어요?
Did you like that movie?

Kkot-eul joahaseyo?
꽃을 좋아하세요?
Do you like the flowers?

Agideul-eun uyu-reul joahaeyo.
아기들은 우유를 좋아해요.
Babies like milk.

Goyangi-do uyu-reul joahaji annayo?
고양이도 우유를 좋아하지 않나요?
Don't cats like milk, too?

To say *I like something* you can use the above expression, or you can use a somewhat weaker (and more sophisticated) expression which means something like *as for me, the thing is liked*:

Na-neun geu yeonghwa-ga joayo.
나는 그 영화가 좋아요.
I like that movie.

Na-neun yeogi-ga joayo.
나는 여기가 좋아요.
I like this place.

Na-neun i eumsik-i joayo.
나는 이 음식이 좋아요.
I like this food.

Na neun Ilbon eul joa haet sseoyo.
나는 일본을 좋아했어요.
I liked Japan.

The verb **joayo** has three meanings: (1) *is good*, (2) *is liked*, (3) *am happy*.

The expression **joahaeyo** has two meanings: (1) *likes*, (2) *is happy*.

Notice that the THING you like takes the particle **i/ga** with the expression **joayo**; but the particle **eul/reul** is more common with **joahaseyo**.

To say *I like* TO DO *something* you have to use a special form of the verb in front of **joayo** or **joahaeyo**. This is the **-gi** form. The ending is added to the bases just like the gerund (**-go**) form:

Na-neun yeonghwa bogi-reul joahaeyo.
나는 영화 보기를 좋아해요.
I like to see movies.

Aideul-eun seonmul bakki joahaeyo.

아이들은 선물 받기 좋아해요.

The children like to get presents.

Harabeoji-kkeseo yeohaeng-eul joahasyeosseoyo.

할아버지께서 여행을 좋아 하셨어요.

My grandfather used to like making trips.

Jungguk eumsik jeom-eseo deusigil joahaeyo?

중국 음식점에서 드시길 좋아하세요?

Do you like to eat in Chinese restaurants?

Notice that *I* WOULD LIKE *to* is not the same as *I* LIKE *to*.

I WOULD *like to* means *I* WANT *to* = **-go sipeoyo**.

I LIKE *to* means *it is pleasant for me to* = **-gi joahaeyo**.

You may be puzzled why you don't hear the **h** in **joahaeyo** and **noayo**. **H** between voiced sounds frequently disappears, and in verb forms like these it usually isn't pronounced at all. You may even hear a **w**-like sound between the **o** and **a** and want to write the words **joayo** and **noayo**.

LESSON 32

Infinitive + *seo* = "And So"

When the particle **seo** follows the infinitive, the meaning is something like *does and so, is and so* or just *does and, is and*:

Don-i eopseoseo mot gayo.
돈이 없어서 못가요.
I haven't any money so I can't go.

This could be broken up into two shorter sentences with the connective expression **geuraeseo**:

Don-i eopseoyo. Geuraeseo mot gayo.
돈이 없어요. 그래서 못가요.
I don't have money. So I can't go.

For the past—*did and so, was and so*—you usually just use the plain infinitive plus **seo**, since the final verb shows that the meaning is past. There is a past infinitive (**-eosseo, -asseo** etc.) which can be used to make the pastness explicit:

Bae-ga gopaseo bap meogeureo gasseoyo.
배가 고파서 밥 먹으러 갔어요.
I was hungry so I went into the restaurant.

(**Bae** = *stomach*. **Bae gopayo** = *is hungry*. The base of **gopayo** is **gopeu-**.)

Mok-i mallaseo mul-eul masyoesseoyo.

목이 말라서 물을 마셨어요.

I was thirsty so I drank some water.

(**Mok** = *throat*, **Mallayo** = *gets dry, is dry. Drinks is either* **meogeoyo** *or* **masyeoyo**; *the base of* **masyeoyo** *is* **masi-**.)

Here are some more examples:

Hanguk yeoksa-reul gongbu hago sipeoseo Seoul Daehak-e danigo isseoyo.

한국 역사를 공부하고싶어요. 서울 대학에 다니고 있어요.

I want to study Korea's history, so I am going to Seoul University.

(**Danyeoyo** = *goes regularly, goes back and forth, keeps going.* Base is **dani-**.)

Jigeum jip-e gaya haeseo taeksi-reul japko isseoyo.

지금집에 가야 해서 택시를 잡고 있어요.

I have to go home now, so I am looking for a taxi.

Kkot-eul joahaeseo nal-mada gongwon-e sanchaekgayo.

꽃을 좋아해서 날마다 공원에 산책가요.

I like flowers, so I take a walk in the park every day.

Hakgyo-ga meoreoseo georeogal su eopseoyo.

학교가 멀어서 걸어갈 수 없어요.

My school is far away so I can't walk.

Hakgyo-ga jip-eseo gakkawoseo georeo danyeoyo.

학교가 집에서 가까워서 걸어 다녀요.

My school is near (from) the house, so I can walk.

(**Georeogayo** = *walks, goes on foot.* **Georeowayo** = *walks, comes on foot.*)

Gongwon-i gakkapji anaseo, jeoncheol-lo gaya haeyo.

공원이 가깝지 않아서 전철로 가야해요.

The park isn't near, so I have to go by subway.

Uri jip-i jeonggeojang-eseo meolji anaseo, georeowado dweyo.

우리집이 정거장에서 멀지 않아서걸어와도 되요.

Our house isn't far from the station, so I can come from there on foot.

Taeksi tal piryo eopseoyo.

택시 탈 필요 없어요.

You don't have to take a taxi.

Gicha tago ogo sipeojjiman gicha-ga eopsesseoyo.

기차 타고 오고 싶었지만 기차가 없었어요.

I want to come (riding) on a train, but there wasn't any.

Taeksi-reul tago dora gaseyo.

택시 타고돌아가세요.

Go home in a cab.

(**Tayo** = *takes (a vehicle)*. **Tagogayo** = *goes in (a vehicle)*. **Tagowayo** = *comes in (a vehicle)*. Compare: **Bihaenggi ro wasseoyo.** = *I came by plane*. **Bihaenggi-reul tago wasseoyo.** = *I came on a plane*.)

The infinitive plus **seo** means *does and* in expressions like *goes and does* or *comes and does*:

Gage-e gaseo gwail-eul sasseoyo.

가게에 가서 과일을 샀어요.

He went to the store and bought some fruit.

Oneul achim-e doseogwan-e gaseo, chaek-eul billil geo eyo.

오늘 아침에 도서관에 가서, 책을 빌릴 거에요.

This morning I'm going to the library (building) and borrow a book.

The expression **joayo** means *I'm glad that*; **joa haseyo** means *someone else is glad that*:

Geu yeonghwa-reul bogoseo aideul-i joahaesseoyo.

그 영화를 보고서 아이들이 좋아 했어요.

The children were glad they saw that movie.

I chaek ilkkoseo joasseoyo.

이 책 읽고서 좋았어요.

I'm glad I read this book.

Hangungmal-eul baewoseo joayo?

한국말을 배워서 좋아요?

Are you glad you studied Korean?

Adeul-i siheom-e hapgyeok haeseo joayo.

아들이 시험에 합격해서 좋아요.

I'm glad my son passed the exam.

Uri hakgyo doseogwan-e chaek-i manaseo haksaengdeul-i joahaeyo.

우리 학교 도서관에 책이 많아서 학생들이 좋아해요.

The students are happy that our school library room has quite a few books (… that the books are not few).

Some Peculiar Verb Types

Verb bases with the basic form ending in **w** change this **w** to **p** or **u** in certain forms:

doum	도움	to help
dowayo	도와요	helps
dopji anayo	돕지 않아요	doesn't help
dopgo isseoyo	돕고 있어요	is helping
douseyo	도우세요	(someone honored) helps
dopko geseyo or **dousigo geseyo**		(someone honored) is helping
돕고 계세요 OR 도우시고 계세요		

Here are some of these verbs:

nuwoyo	누워요	lies down
swiwoyo	쉬워요	is easy
eoryeowoyo	어려워요	is difficult
chuwoyo	추워요	is cold
kakkawoyo	가까워요	is near
areumdawoyo	아름다워요	is beautiful
yeppeoyo	예뻐요	is pretty
deowoyo	더워요	is hot
maewoyo	매워요	is hot-tasting, spicy
bangawoyo	반가워요	is glad to meet you
gomawoyo	고마워요	is grateful

Most of these verbs correspond to English adjectives; they mean IS *something* rather than DOES *something*.

Verb bases ending in **l** or **r** are of two types: regular consonant **r-** bases, and **l-** extending vowel bases. In the first type, the **r** is replaced (by **jj**, **g**, **kk**) in certain forms:

geor- 걸어–	to walk
georeoyo 걸어요	walks
geojji anayo 걷지 않아요	doesn't walk
geokko isseoyo 걷고 있어요	is walking
georeuseyo 걸으세요	(someone honored) walks
geokko geseyo or **georeusigo geseyo** 걷고 계세요 OR 걸으시고 계세요	(someone honored) is walking

In the second type, the **l** (or **r**) is an extension which the base acquires before you attach certain endings:

georeo- 걸어–	to hang
georeoyo 걸어요	hangs
geolji anayo 걸지 않아요	doesn't hang
geolgo isseoyo 걸고 있어요	is hanging
geoseyo 거세요	(someone honored) hangs
geolgo geseyo or **geosigo geseyo** 걸고 계세요 OR 거시고 계세요	(someone honored) is hanging

You will notice that some of the forms of the consonant **r-** bases are the same as those of the **l-** extending vowel bases:

	CONSONANT BASE	VOWEL BASE	CONSONANT BASE	VOWEL BASE
BASE	geor- to *walk*	geo-l- to *hang*	deur- to *listen*	deur- to *enter*
PRESENT	georeoyo	georeoyo	deureoyo	deureowayo
PAST	georeo- sseoyo	georeo- sseoyo	deureo- sseoyo	deureo- waseoyo
HON.	georeuseyo	geoseyo	deureoseyo	deureooseyo
HON. PAST	georeusye- sseoyo	geosye- sseoyo	deureusyeo- sseoyo	deureoosyeo- sseoyo
-JI	geojji	geolji	deutchi	deureooji
GERUND	geokko	geolgo	deutkko	deureoogo

Here are some consonant bases ending in **r**:

mur- = to inquire	**mureoyo, mutji anayo, mukko** 물어요, 묻지 않아요, 묻고
dalr- = to run	**dalyeoyo, daliji anayo, daligo** 달려요, 달리지 않아요, 달리고
sir- = to be loaded with	**sireoyo, sijji anayo, sikko** 실어요, 싣지 않아요, 싣고
kkaedar- = realize	**kkaedarayo, kkaedajji anayo, kkaedakko** 깨달아요, 깨닫지 않아요, 깨닫고

Here are some **l-** extending vowel bases:

gil- = to be long	**gireoyo, gilji anayo, gilgo** 길어요, 길지 않아요, 길고
al- = to know, find out	**arayo, algo** 알아요, 알고
sal- = to live	**sarayo, salji anayo, salgo** 살아요, 살지 않아요, 살고
ul- = to cry	**ureoyo, ulji anayo, ulgo** 울어요, 울지 않아요, 울고
nol- = to play, visit, enjoy	**norayo, nolji anayo, nolgo** 놀아요, 놀지 않아요, 놀고
yeol- = to open	**yeoreoyo, yeolji anayo, yeol go**

열어요, 열지 않아요, 열고

bul- = to blow   **bureoyo, bulji anayo, bulgo**

불어요, 불지 않아요, 불고

ppal- = to launder   **pparayo, ppalji anayo, ppalgo**

빨아요, 빨지 않아요, 빨고

NOTE: The negative of **arayo** is a special verb **mollayo** = *does not know*.
(Base = **moreu-**.) Examples of some of these verbs follow:

Je-ga gil-eul molaseo gyeongchal-ege mureo bwasseoyo.
제가 길을 몰라서 경찰에게 물어 봤어요.
I didn't know the road, so I asked (tried inquiring of) a policeman.

Gildong i-ga abeoji sori-reul deukko dalyeo wasseoyo.
길동이가 아버지 소리를 듣고 달려 왔어요.
Kildong heard his father's voice and came running.

Ulji maseyo.
울지마세요
Don't cry.

Geugeot-eul kkaedajji mot haesseoyo.
그것을 깨닫지 못했어요.
I hadn't realized that.

Nugu-hante deureosseoyo?
누구한테 들었어요?
Who did you find that out from?

Dowa juseyo.
도와 주세요
Help me.

Nal-i neomu deowoseo jago sipeoyo.
날이 너무 더워서 자고 싶어요.
The weather (day) is too warm, so I want to sleep. The weather is SO
warm I want to sleep.

Neomu chuwoseo koteu-reul ibeoya haeyo.

너무 추워서 코트를 입어야 해요.

The weather is so cold. You have to wear an overcoat.

Hangungmal-i swipji anayo.

한국말이 쉽지 않아요.

Korean isn't easy.

Yeongeo-do eoryeowoyo.

영어도 어려워요.

English is difficult, too.

I eumsik-i neomu maewo seo, mot meok gesseoyo.

이 음식이 너무 매워서, 못 먹겠어요.

This food is so hot-tasting, I can't eat it.

Mannaseo, cham bangawoyo.

만나서 참 반가워요.

I am very happy to meet you.

The Modifiers *-eun* and *-n*

In English we have expressions like *the man* THAT *came yesterday* or *the man* WHO *came yesterday*, *the man* THAT *I saw yesterday* or *the man* WHO(M) *I saw yesterday*. These are called relative clauses and usually contain a relative pronoun—*who, which, that, where*—though this is sometimes omitted: *the man I saw yesterday*.

In the equivalent Korean expression, there is no relative pronoun, and the relative clause goes in front of the noun it modifies; you say something like *the came-yesterday man, the I-saw-yesterday man*. The verb in these modifying constructions appears in a special form we shall call the MODIFIER form.

The ordinary modifier form has the ending **-eun** after a consonant base, **-n** after a vowel base:

anjeun saram	앉은 사람	the man who sat down
on saram	온 사람	the man who came

The meaning of the modifier form depends on whether the Korean verb corresponds to an English verb or an English adjective; in other words, whether the verb means DOES *something* or IS *something*. The meaning of the modifier form with PROCESS verbs (*does something*) is ...*that has done* or ...*that someone has done*: **bon saram** = *the man that saw* or *the man that someone saw*.

To make it clear which of these two meanings is involved you have to give the verb either a subject or an object:

Gim seonsaeng-eul bon saram.

김 선생을 본 사람.

The man that saw Mr. Kim.

Gim seonsaeng-i bon saram.

김 선생이 본 사람.

The man that Mr. Kim saw.

Then you can take the whole expression and make it the subject, or the object of a larger sentence, by putting an appropriate particle after the noun:

Gim seonsaeng-i bon saram-i nae chingu eyo.

김 선생이 본 사람이 내 친구에요.

The man Mr. Kim saw is my friend.

Gim seonsaeng-eul bon saram-i nae chingu eyo.

김 선생을 본 사람이 내 친구에요.

The man who saw Mr. Kim is my friend.

Gim seonsaeng-i bon saram-eul na-do bwasseoyo.

김 선생이 본 사람을 나도 봤어요.

I too saw the man Mr. Kim saw.

Gim seonsaeng-eul bon saram-i na-reul bwasseoyo.

김 선생을 본 사람이 나를 봤어요.

The man who saw Mr. Kim saw me too.

Gim seonsaeng-i bon saram-hante don-eul badasseoyo.

김 선생이 본 사람한테 돈을 받았어요.

Mr. Kim got money from the man he saw. (Also could mean: I got money from the man Mr. Kim saw.)

Gim seonsaeng-eul bon saram-hante (Gim seonsaeng-i) don-eul badasseoyo.

김 선생을 본 사람한테 (김 선생이) 돈을 받았어요.

Mr. Kim got money from the man who saw him.

Compare the following sets of sentences:

Geu saram-i doseogwan-eseo chaek-uel billyeosseoyo.
그 사람이 도서관에서 책을 빌렸어요.
That person borrowed a book from the library.

Doseogwan-eseo chaek-eul billin saram-i nugu eyo?
도서관에서 책을 빌린 사람이 누구에요?
Who was the person who borrowed a book from the library?

Geu saram-i doseogwan-eseo billin chaek-i museun chaek ieyo?
그 사람이 도서관에서 빌린 책이 무슨 책이에요?
What was the book that person borrowed from the library?

Geu-ga mun-eul dadasseoyo.
그 남자가 문을 닫았어요.
The man closed the door.

The meaning of the modifier form with DESCRIPTION verbs (*is something*) is simply *...that is:*

keun jip	큰 집	a house that is big = a big house
meon dosi	먼 도시	a city that is far away = a far-away city
gakkaun hakgyo	가까운 학교	a school that is nearby = a nearby school
jeolmeun saram	젊은 사람	a person who is young = a young person
moksa in bun	목사인 분	a(n honored) man who is a preacher
gin gil	긴 길	a road that is long = a long road
jjalbeun gil	짧은 길	a road that is short = a short road
ppalgan moja	빨간 모자	a hat that is red = a red hat
hin ot	흰 옷	clothes that are white = white clothes
geomeun gudu	검은 구두	black shoes
pureun haneul	푸른 하늘	blue sky

joeun nal	좋은 날	nice day, nice weather
nappeun nalssi	나쁜 날씨	bad weather
nopeun san	높은 산	high mountains
najeun eondeok	낮은 언덕	low hill
chuun bam	추운 밤	a cold night
jageun ai	작은 아이	a small child

These expressions can then be made the subject, or the object of larger sentences.

The possibilities, you can see, are endless. In Lesson 35 you will find a list of modifiers for typical verb shapes.

The Verb Modifier *-neun*

Bwayo means either *looks at, sees* or *reads*. (*Sees a person* is often translated as **mannayo** = *meets*.) But to say *the man who is reading* or *the book that the man is reading* you can't use **bon** because **bon saram** means *the man who has read* and **bon chaek** means *the book someone has read*.

Instead, there is a special form, the PROCESSIVE modifier, used only with process verbs (DOES *something*). This form is made by adding the ending **-neun** to the verb base. (Various sound changes take place automatically when you attach the ending to a consonant base.) So we have sentences like:

Chaek-eul ilkko inneun saram-i nugu eyo?
책을 읽고 있는 사람이 누구에요?
Who is the man (who is) reading the book?

Chaek bogo inneun saram mannan jeok isseoyo?
책 보고 있는 사람 만난 적 있어요?
Have you met the man who is reading the book? Did you see a man reading a book?

Geu saram-i boneun chaek-i museun chaek ieyo?
그 사람이 보는 책이 무슨 책이에요?
What is the book he is reading?

Geu saram-i boneun chaek na-do bwasseoyo.
그 사람이 보는 책 나도 봤어요.
I too have read the book he is reading.

For some verbs *does* is a better translation than *is doing*:

Satang-eul johahaneun yeohaksaeng.
사탕을 좋아하는 여학생.
A girl who likes candy.

Jipe gago sipeohaneun ai.
집에 가고 싶어하는 아이.
The child who wants to go home.

Notice that the **-neun** modifier form is not used with DESCRIPTION verbs (*is something*)—these have only the **-eun** form. This is why the **-eun** modifier comes out with two different translations: *which* HAS DONE for process verbs and *which* IS for description verbs. You will sometimes be in doubt whether a particular verb is a process or a description verb; but the English translation usually tells you.

   Isseoyo and **eopseoyo** are a bit strange; they sometimes behave like description verbs, sometimes like process verbs. The forms **isseun** and **eopseum** are rare, however: one usually hears only **inneun** ...*that exists, that someone has* and **oemneun** ...*that is nonexistent, that someone doesn't have*.

   Here is a list of some typical verb bases with their modifier forms:

I. CONSONANT BASES

MEANING	BASE	-EUN	-NEUN
catches	**jab-** 잡	**abeun** 잡은	**jamneun** 잡는
is high	**nop-** 높	**nopeun** 높은	–
is nonexistent	**eops-** 없	**(eopseun)**	**eomneun** 없는
closes	**dad** 닫	**dadeun** 닫은	**danneun** 닫는
is like	**gat-** 같	**gateun** 같은	–
laughs	**us-** 웃	**useun** 웃은	**uneun** 웃는

MEANING	BASE	-EUN	-NEUN
exists	**iss-** 있	**(isseun)** 있은	**inneun** 있는
finds	**chaj** 찾	**chajeun** 찾은	**channeun** 찾는
washes	**ssis-** 씻	**ssiseun** 씻은	**ssinneun** 씻는
reads	**ilk-** 읽	**ilgeun** 읽은	**ilneun** 읽는
loses	**ilh-** 잃	**ireun** 잃은	**ireun** 잃는
licks	**halt-** 핥	**halteun** 핥은	**halleun** 핥는
steps on	**balb-** 밟	**balbeun** 밟은	**bamneun** 밟는
puts	**noh-** 놓	**noeun** 놓은	**nonneun** 놓는
eats	**meok-** 먹	**meogeun** 먹은	**meongneun** 먹는
cuts	**kkakk-** 깎	**kkakkeun** 깎은	**kkangneun** 깎는
shampoos	**gam-** 감	**gameun** 감은	**gamneun** 감는
is young	**jeolm-** 젊	**jolmeun** 젊은	**–**
wears on feet	**sin-** 신	**sineun** 신은	**sinneun** 신는
sits	**anj-** 앉	**anjeun** 앉은	**anneun** 앉는
breaks	**breojin-** 부러진	**breojineun** 부러지는	**breojin** 부러진

II. VOWEL BASES

is, equals	**(i)-**	**(i)-n**	**–**
honorific	**-(eu)si-** 시	**-(eu)sin** 신	**-(eu)sineun** 시는
rests	**swi-** 쉬	**swin** 쉰	**swineun** 쉬는

MEANING	BASE	-EUN	-NEUN
becomes	dwe- 되	dwen 된	dweneun 되는
pays	nae- 내	naen 낸	naeneun 내는
writes	sseu- 쓰	sseun 쓴	sseuneun 쓰는
goes	ga- 가	gan 간	ganeun 가는
gives	ju- 주	jun 준	juneun 주는
sees, reads	bo- 보	bon 본	boneun 보는
does	ha- 하	han 한	haneun 하는
calls	bureu- 부르	bureun 부른	bureuneun 부르는

III. -W BASES

helps	dow- 도	doun 도운	domneun 돕는
lies	nuw- 누	nuun 누운	numneun 눕는
is near	gakkaw 가까우	gakkaun 가까운	–
is pretty	yepp- 예	yeppeun 예쁜	–

IV. -R BASES

walks	geor- 걸	–	geonneun 걷는
listens	deur- 들	–	deureooneun 들어오는

V. L- EXTENDING VOWEL BASES

hangs	geo-l- 걸	geon 건	keoneun 거는
enters	deu-l- 들	deun 든	deuneun 드는

Ever, Never and Sometimes

The modifier forms are used in a number of handy expressions best learned as units:

-eun il-i isseoyo
−은 일이 있어요
has done, (once) did, has done indeed

-eun il-i isseosseoyo
−은 일이 있었어요
had ever, once had done

-eun il-i eopseoyo
−은 일이 없어요
has never, never did

-eun il-i eopseosseoyo
−은 일이 없었어요
had never, never had done

The noun **il** means *work*, *job* but it also means *act*, *experience*—so the literal meaning of the above expressions is something like *the act or experience of having done something exists* (or *doesn't exist*). Here are some examples:

Hanguk eumsik-eul meogeo bon jeok-i isseoyo?
한국 음식을 먹어 본적이 있어요?
Have you ever tried eating Korean food?

Isseoyo.
있어요
Yes, I have.

Hanguk eumsikjeom-eseo meogeun jeok isseoyo.
한국 음식점에서 먹은 적 있어요.
Yes, I have. I've been to a Korean restaurant to eat.

Geu gongwon-e sanchaek gan jeok isseoyo?
그 공원에 산책 간 적 있어요?
Have you ever taken a walk in that park?

Eojet bam-e cheoeum-euro geu gongwon-eseo sanchaek-eul haesseoyo.
어젯 밤에 처음으로 그 공원에서 산책을 했어요
Up to yesterday I hadn't ever taken a walk in that park, but yesterday I went there and took a walk.

Miguk yeonghwa-reul bon jeok i eopseoyo?
미국 영화를 본적이 없어요?
Haven't you ever seen an American movie?

Geureoke joeun eumak-eul deureun jeog-i eopseoyo.
그렇게 좋은 음악을 들은 적이 없어요
I've never heard such pretty music.

Now learn the following expressions:

-neun il-i isseoyo –는 일이 있어요	sometimes does, does indeed (on occasion)
-neun il-i isseosseoyo –는 일이 있었어요	sometimes did, would indeed do
-neun il-i eopseoyo –는 일이 없어요	never does, doesn't ever do
-neun il-i eopseosseoyo –는 일이 없었어요	never would do, never used to do

These expressions mean literally *the act or experience of doing exists* (or *does not exist*). Here are some examples:

Dambae-neun gakkeum pijiman, sul-eul masineun il-eun eopseoyo.
담배는 가끔 피지만 술을 마시는 일은 없어요.
He sometimes smokes, but he never drinks.

Nan-eun sul-eul masigineun hajiman, neomu masyeoseo jamdeuneun il-eun eopseoyo.
나는 술을 마시기는 하지만 너무 많이 마셔서 잠드는 일은 없어요.
I sometimes drink, but I've never drunk so much that I've fallen asleep.

Before, After and While

To say *before something happens* or *before something happened* you use the **-gi** form followed by **jeon** = *prior, earlier, before, ago* usually followed by the particle **e**:

Hakgyo gagi jeon-e gongbu-reul haeyo.
학교 가기 전에 공부를 해요.
I study the lesson before I come to school.

Biga ogi jeon-e jip-e gaya haeyo.
비가 오기 전에 집에 가야 해요.
I've got to get home before it rains.

Yeonseol-eul sijak hagi jeon-e, mul-eul masyeoya haeyo.
연설을 시작하기 전에 물을 마셔야 해요.
Before beginning my speech I take a drink of water.

Jip-eseo tteonagi jeon-e jeo-hante jeonhwa juseyo.
집에서 떠나기 전에 저한테 전화 주세요.
Please phone me before you leave (go out of) your house.

To say *after something happens* or *after something happened* you use the ordinary modifier form **-eun** plus **hu** = *afterward* which may be followed by the particle **e**:

Jip-e on hu-e gongbu haesseoyo.
집에 온 후에 공부했어요.
I studied after I came home.

Yeonghwa-reul bon hu-e kape-eseo cha han jan masyeosseoyo.
영화를 본 후에 카페에서 차 한 잔 마셨어요.
After we had watched the movie, we went to a cafe and drank a cup of (black) tea.

Uri gae-ga jugeun hu-e aideul-i oraet dongan ureosseoyo.
우리 개가 죽은후에 아이들이 오랫동안 울었어요.
After our dog died, the children cried for a long time.
(**orae** = *long time*; **dongan** = *interval*)

Yeonghwa-reul bon hu-e baro jip-euro doraoseyo.
영화를 본 후에 바로 집으로 돌아 오세요.
Come right back home after you have seen the movie.

Dangsin-i jam jagi jeon-e doduk-i deureo wasseoyo, jam deun hu-e deureo wasseoyo?
당신이 잠 자기 전에 도둑이 들어왔어요, 잠 잔 후에 들어왔어요?
Did the thief come in after you had gone to bed, (or) before you went to bed?

To say *while something is happening* you use the processive modifier **-neun** followed by **jung** = *in the midst of*, or **dongan** = *interval*, or **sai** (**sae**) = *interval*. The particle **e** may follow:

Jam jago itteon jung ieosseoyo.
잠자고 있던 중 이었어요.
It was while we were sleeping.

Dangsin-i malhago inneun dongan jeo-neun juwi gipke deukko itsseoyo.
당신이 말하고 있는 동안 저는 주의깊게 듣고 있어요.
While you were talking I was listening closely (well).

Jeo-neun jigeum gongbu jung igo gongbu kkeunnamyeon sanchaek gal geoeyo.

저는 지금 공부 중이고 공부 끝나면 산책 갈 거에요.

I am now in the midst of studying but after I've studied, I am going to take a walk.

Dangsin-i sanchaek naga inneun dongan sonnim-i chaja osyeos-seoyo.

당신이 산책 나가 있는 동안 손님이 찾아 오셨어요.

While you were walking, a guest came to the house.

In the Future

The ordinary present form of verbs often has a future meaning:

Naeil hakgyo-e gayo.
내일 학교에 가요.
I'm going to school tomorrow.

But if you want to make the future specific, or if you want to refer to a probable present (especially with adjectives), you can use the **gesseoyo** form.

This **-gesseyo** is added to the verb base in the same way **-go** and **-gi** are added:

Bi-ga ogi jeon-e usan-eul saya gesseoyo.
비가 오기 전에 우산을 사야 겠어요
I'll have to buy an umbrella before it rains.

Naeil byeongwon-e ga bwaya gesseoyo.
내일 병원에 가 봐야 겠어요.
I'll have to go to a doctor.

Mueot-eul deusigesseoyo?
무엇을 드시겠어요?
What will we eat?

Miguk-e doragasimyeon, mueot-eul hasigo sipeuseyo?
미국에 돌아가시면 무엇을 하시고 싶으세요?
What will you do when you get back to America?

Eodi-seo sasil geon gayo?
어디서 사실 건가요?
Where will you live?

Eonje Hanguk-e doraosil geon gayo?
언제 한국에 돌아 오실 건가요?
When will you return to Korea?

Notice the difference between **Jigwon-i jigeum il-eul hago isseul geoyeyo**, *The factory-worker must be working now* and **Jigwon-i jigeum il-eul haeya haeyo**, *The factory-worker must work now*. Sometimes *must* means *likely, probably*; sometimes it means *has to*.

There is also a FUTURE MODIFIER form meaning *…that will do* or *…that someone will do* or *…that is to be done*:

Sseul pyeonji-ga isseoyo.
쓸 편지가 있어요
I have letters to write.

I il-eul hal saram-i isseoyo?
이 일을 할 사람이 있어요?
Is there someone (a person) to do this job?

Jeo-reul annae haejul saram-eul chakko isseoyo.
저를 안내해 줄내할 사람을 찾고 있어요.
I'm looking for someone to show me around (guide me).

Mueot-eul bosigesseoyo?
무엇을 보시겠어요.
What are you (going) to see?

Meogeul geot-i isseoyo?
먹을 것이 있어요?
Is there anything to eat?

Je-ga meogeul geot-i innayo?
제가 먹을 것이 있나요?
Would there (likely) be anything for me to eat?

Eomma-ga jeonyeok-eul junbi hago isseul geoeyo.
엄마가 저녁을 준비하고 있을 거예요.
My mother must be cooking dinner for us.

Uri-neun geunyeo-ui saengil pati-reul junbi haeya haeyo.
우리는 그녀의 생일 파티를 준비해야 해요.
We must prepare for her birthday party.

Halmeoni-kkeseo nae keik eul mandeusigo gyeseyo.
할머니께서 내 케익을 만드시고 계세요.
My grandmother is making my birthday cake.

Uri-neun geunyeo-ui seonmul-eul saya haeyo.
우리는 그녀의 선물을 사야 해요.
We must buy her present.

The ending of the future modifier form is **-eul** after a consonant base, **-l** after a vowel base. Here are some typical verb types, with future and future modifier forms:

I. CONSONANT BASES

MEANING	BASE	-GESSEOYO	-EUL/-L
catches	**jab-** 잡	**japgesseoyo** 잡겠어요	**jabeul** 잡을
is high	**nop-** 높	**nopgesseoyo** 높겠어요	**nopeul** 높을
is nonexistent	**eops-** 없	**eopgesseoyo** 없겠어요	**eopseul** 없을
closes	**dad-** 닫	**dakkesseoyo** 닫겠어요	**dadeul** 닫을

MEANING	BASE	-GESSEOYO	-EUL/-L
is like	gat- 같	gakkesseoyo 같겠어요	gateul 같을
laughs	us- 웃	ukkesseoyo 웃겠어요	useul 웃을
exist	iss- 있	ikkesseoyo 있겠어요	isseul 있을
finds	chaj- 찾	chakkesseoyo 찾겠어요	chajeul 찾을
washes	ssich- 씻	ssikkesseoyo 씻겠어요	ssiseul 씻을
reads	ilg- 읽	ilkkesseoyo 읽겠어요	ilgeul 읽을
loses	ji- 지	jigeseoyo 지겠어요	jil 질
licks	halt- 핥	halkkesseoyo 핥겠어요	halteul 핥을
steps on	balb- 밟	balkkesseoyo 밟겠어요	balbeul 밟을
puts	noh- 놓	nokesseoyo 놓겠어요	noeul 놓을
eats	meog- 먹	meokkesseoyo 먹겠어요	meogeul 먹을
cuts	kkakk- 깎	kkakkesseoyo 깎겠어요	kkakkeul 깎을
shampoos	gam- 감	gamkkesseoyo 감겠어요	gameul 감을
wears on feet	sin- 신	sinkkesseoyo 신겠어요	sineul 신을
sits	anj- 앉	ankkesseoyo 앉겠어요	anjeul 앉을
breaks	busu- 부수	busugesseoyo 부수겠어요	busul 부술
is, equals	(i)- 이	-(i)gesseoyo (이)겠어요	(i)-l 을
honorific	-(eu)si- (으)시	-(eu)sigesseoyo (으)시겠어요	-(eu)sil (으)실

II. VOWEL BASES

MEANING	BASE	-GESSEOYO	-EUL/-L
rests	swi- 쉬	swigesseoyo 쉬겠어요	swil 쉴
becomes	dwe- 되	dwegesseoyo 되겠어요	dwel 될
pays	nae- 내	naegesseoyo 내겠어요	nael 낼
writes	sseu- 쓰	sseugesseoyo 쓰겠어요	sseul 쓸
goes	ga- 가	gagesseoyo 가겠어요	gal 갈
gives	ju- 주	jugesseoyo 주겠어요	jul 줄
sees	bo- 보	bogesseoyo 보겠어요	bol 볼
does	ha- 하	hagesseoyo 하겠어요	hal 할
calls	bureu- 부르	bureugesseoyo 부르겠어요	bureul 부를

III. -W BASES

helps	dow- 도	dopgesseoyo 돕겠어요	doul 도울
lies down	nuw- 누	nupgesseoyo 눕겠어요	nuul 누울
is near	gakkaw- 가까우	gakkapgesseoyo 가깝겠어요	gakkaul 가까울
buy	saw- 사	sagesseoyo 사겠어요	sal 살

IV. -R BASES

MEANING	BASE	-GESSEOYO	-EUL/-L
walks	geor- 걸	geokkesseoyo 걷겠어요	georeul 걸을
listens	deur- 듣	deukkesseoyo 듣겠어요	deureul 들을

V. **L-** EXTENDING VOWEL BASES

MEANING	BASE	-GESSEOYO	-EUL/-L
hangs	**geo-l-**	**geolgesseoyo**	**geol**
	걸	걸겠어요	걸
enters	**deul-**	**deureogagesseoyo**	**deul**
	들	들어가겠어요	들

"Knows" and "Can"

To say someone *knows* something or someone, you use the verb **arayo** (**a-l-**); the negative of this is a special verb, **mollayo** (**moreu-**) *does not know*. These verbs are often used with the FUTURE **gesseoyo**, even though the English translation uses the present:

Arayo?
알아요?
Do you know?

Geu-neun moreujiman geu saram abeoji-neun arayo.
그는 모르지만 그 사람 아버지는 알아요.
I don't know him but I know his father. (Also could mean: He doesn't know but his father knows.)

You will recall that the future sometimes means just a PROBABLE PRESENT. Notice the deferential way in English we say:

Gicha-ga tteonaneun sigan arayo?
기차가 떠나는 시간 알아요?
Would you know what time the train leaves?

Seoul-e dochak haneun sigan-eul moreugesseoyo.
서울 에 도착하는 시간을 모르겠어요
I wouldn't know what time it gets to Seoul.

(**tteonada-** = *leave*, **dochak hada-** = *arrive*.)

To say someone *knows* THAT something happened, you say someone *knows* the FACT (**geot**) that something happened:

Gitcha-ga beolsseo tteonan geo aseyo?
기차가 벌써 떠난 거 아세요?
Do you know (realize) that the train has already left?

Note: The verb **arayo** sometimes means *realizes, finds out.*

To say someone *knows* HOW TO do something, you use the future modifier **-eul** followed by the word **jul** and **arayo**:

Yeongeo hal jul aseyo?
영어 할 줄 아세요?
Do you know how to speak English? Can you speak English?

Hangukmal eul jal hal jul mollayo.
한국말을 잘 할 줄 몰라요.
I don't know how to speak Korean very well.

Hangeul-eul sseul jul moreujiman, gongbu hago sipeunde gareuchy-eo juseyo.
한글을 쓸 줄 모르지만, 공부하고 싶은데 가르쳐 주세요.
I don't know how to write Korean script (**Hangeul**) but I want to study it, so please teach (**gareuchi-**) me a little.

Suyeong hasil jul aseyo?
수영 하실 줄 아세요?
Do you know how to swim?

(**suyeong-** = *swim,* **suyeong haeyo** = *swims.*)

You will notice that this expression **-eul jjul arayo** (and its negative **-eul jjul mollayo**) is sometimes translated *knows how to* (*doesn't know how to*) and sometimes *can* (*can't*).

This is a special meaning of the English word *can;* the more general meaning *is able to, is in a position to* is expressed in Korean by the expression: **-eul hal su isseoyo.** The literal meaning of this expression is something like *there exists the possibility to do:*

Hangeul-eul sseul jul aljiman, pen-i eopseoseo, jigeum-eun sseul su eopseoyo.

한글을 쓸 줄 알지만 펜이 없어서 지금은 쓸 수 없어요.

I know how to write Korean letters but I haven't a pen, so I can't write (them) right now.

Sigan-i eopseoseo chungbunhi gongbu hal su eopseosseoyo.

시간이 없어서 충분히 공부 할 수 없었어요.

I didn't have any time, so I couldn't study enough.

Sigan-eun ijjiman don-i eopseoseo chingu mannareo nagal su-ga eopseoyo.

시간은 있지만 돈이 없어서 친구 만나러 갈수가 없어요.

I've got the time, but I haven't any money so I can't go out to meet my friends.

There is still a third meaning of *can*—the same as the word *may*:

Nae haendeupon-eul sseodo gwaen chanayo.

내 핸드폰을 써도 괜찮아요.

You can (may) use my cell phone (because you have my permission).

Contrast this with:

Nae handeupon-eul sseul su isseoyo.

내 핸드폰을 쓸 수 있어요.

You can (are able to) use my cell phone (because it is working).

Here are some more examples of these expressions:

Oneul bame gonghang-e gaya haneunde jihacheol tago gal su ikkesseoyo?

오늘밤 공항에 가야하는데 지하철 타고 갈 수 있겠어요?

I have to go to the airport tonight, but will I be able to go by subway?

Jadongcha han dae ijjiman, unjeon hal su inneun saram-i inneunji moreugesseoyo.

자동차 한 대 있지만 운전 할 수 있는 사람이 있는지 모르겠어요.

There is a (one) car available, but I don't know that there is anyone who can drive it.

Unjeon hasil jul aseyo?

운전하실 줄 아세요?

Do you know how to drive?

Molla yo. Unjeon hal jul molayo.

몰라요, 운전 할 줄 몰라요.

No I don't, I don't know how to drive.

Geureona uri chingu-ga unjeon hal jul arayo. Geu-ga dangsin-eul deryeoda jul su isseulgeoeyo.

그러나 우리 친구 가 운전할 줄 알아요 그가 당신을 데려다 줄 수 있을 거에요.

But my friend probably knows how to drive. He will be able to take you to the airport.

LESSON 40

Probable Future

The ordinary future **-gesseyo** means either DEFINITE FUTURE or PROBABLE PRESENT. For a probable future (*something probably will happen*) you use the expression **-eul kkeo ieyo** which has a literal meaning somewhat like *it is the likely fact for something to happen*. The word **geot** which has so many meanings—*thing, fact, likely fact, that*—is often shortened to **geo**, and the shortened expression **-eul kkeo eyo** is usually run together to sound like **-eul kkeyo**. Here are some examples of both the full form and the abbreviated form:

will probably catch	**jabeul geo eyo** 잡을거에요	**jabeul kkeyo** 잡을게요
will probably eat	**mogeul geo eyo** 먹을 거에요	**mogeul kkeyo** 먹을게요
will probably read	**ilgeul geo eyo** 읽을 거에요	**ilgeul kkeyo** 읽을게요
will probably come	**ol geo eyo** 올 거에요	**ol kkeyo** 올 게요
will probably live	**sal geo eyo** 살거에요	**sal kkeyo** 살게요

"When" and "If"

There are a number of ways to translate the English word *when*. The most general is perhaps **-eul ttae** = (*at*) *the time when*. The verb in front of **ttae** = *time* is always in the future modifier form regardless of the tense of the English verb:

Beri ullyeoseul ttae naneun jameul jago iseoseoyo.
벨이 울렸을 때 나는 잠을 자고 있었어요.
When the bell rang, I was asleep.

Geu ttae seonsaengnim-eun eodi gyesyesseoyo?
그 때 선생님은 어디 계셨어요?
Where were you then (at that time)?

Bi-ga ol ttae usan-eul gajeogaya haeyo.
비가 올 때 우산을 가져가야 해요.
When it rains, you have to have an umbrella.

Gim seonsaeng jip-e gamyeon, Hangungmal-man hasipsio.
김선생 집에가면 한국말만 하십시오.
When we go to Mr. Kim's house, please speak only Korean.

To say *if* you use a special verb form which has the shape **-myeon** after a consonant base, **-eu myeon** after a vowel base. This is also used to mean *whenever*:

Bi-ga omyeon, jip-e isseul geoeyo.

비가 오면 집에 있을거예요.

If it rains, I'll stay home.

Bi-ga ol ttae myeon, na-neun jip-e isseoyo.

비가 올 때면 나는 집에 있어요.

Whenever it rains, I stay home.

There's a special way to say *when one thing happens then something else interrupts it*—sentences like *when I was listening to the radio, I heard a noise upstairs* or *while we were out walking it rained.*

You use a form which ends in **-da** and is usually followed by the particle **ga**. This shows the single interruption of an action—which may or may not be resumed. **Na neun radio-reul deuddaga, jam-i deureosseoyo.** *I fell asleep while I was listenng to the radio.* **Uriga sanchaek hadaga, bi-reul mannasseoyo.** *While we were taking a walk, the rain came.*

There is a past form of this **-da** which has the ending **-eotta** (or **-atta** with a number of irregularities, like all infinitives and past forms). The meaning of the past **-eotta** form is *when one thing has happened, then something else contradictory or unanticipated happens right after—* without INTERRUPTING the action so much as CHANGING it. For example:

Sangjeom-e gattta wasseoyo.

상점에 갔다 왔어요.

I went to the store and then (turned around and) came right back.

Kim seonsaeng-i ucheguk-e watta gasseoyo.

김 선생이 우체국에 왔다 갔어요

Mr. Kim came to the post office and left again.

Two contradictory actions can be shown as going on in ALTERNATION by using two of these **-eotta** forms followed by **haeyo**:

Saramdeul-i gyesok gwatda gatta haeyo.

사람들이 계속 왔다갔다 해요.

People keep coming and going.

To talk about two actions which are not in alternation, but are going on at the same time, you use the **-eumyeon** form followed by the particle **seo**:

Radio-reul deureumyeonseo gongbu haeyo.
라디오를 들으면서 공부해요.
I study while listening to the radio.

Chaek-eul bomyeonseo agi-reul bwayo.
책을 보면서 아기를봐요.
I read (books) while babysitting.

Sometimes the **-eumyeonseo** form means *even though* (the same as **-eo do**) just as the English *while* can have that meaning:

Hangungmal-eul inyeon jjae gongbu hago isseumyeonseo-do, jal mal hal jul mollayo.
한국말을 이년 째 공부하고 있으면서도 잘 말 할 수 없어요.
While (though) I have been studying Korean for two years, I can't speak it very well.

You may find this a handy tag translation for the **-da(ga)** forms: BUT *then* (*something else happens*).

You will recall that **-eoseo** means *does and then* or *does and so*, and **-go** means *does and then* or *does and also*.

The important thing about the **-da(ga)** forms is that they always show a TRANSFER of action. The gerund **-go** simply links two verb expressions; **-da(ga)** links two verb expressions stressing the CONTRADICTORY nature of the two; **-eoseo** stresses the close CONSEQUENCE of the second verb.

Here are **-eumyeon** and **-da(ga)** forms for some typical verbs:

I. CONSONANT BASES

MEANING	BASE	-EUMYEON, -MYEON	-DA(GA)	-ATTA(GA)
catches	**jab-**	**jabeumyeon**	**japd(ga)**	**jabatta(ga)**
	잡	잡으면	잡다(가)	잡았다(가)
closes	**dad-**	**dadeumyeon**	**datta(ga)**	**dadatta(ga)**
	닫	닫으면	닫다 (가)	닫았다 (가)

MEANING	BASE	-EUMYEON, -MYEON	-DA(GA)	-ATTA(GA)
exists	**iss-** 있	**isseumyeon** 있으면	**itta(ga)** 있다 (가)	**isseotta(ga)** 있었다 (가)
is non-existent	**eops-** 없	**eopseumyeon** 없으면	**eopda(ga)** 없다(가)	**eopseotta(ga)** 없었다(가)
laughs	**us-** 웃	**useumyeon** 웃으면	**utta(ga)** 웃다(가)	**useotta(ga)** 웃었다(가)
finds	**chaj-** 찾	**chajeumyeon** 찾으면	**chatta(ga)** 찾다(가)	**chajatta(ga)** 찾았다(가)
reads	**ilg-** 읽	**ilgeumyeon** 읽으면	**ikda(ga)** 읽다(가)	**ilgeotta(ga)** 읽었다(가)
puts	**noh-** 놓	**noeumyeon** 놓으면	**nota(ga)** 놓다(가)	**noatta(ga)** 놓았다(가)
eats	**meog-** 먹	**meogeumyeon** 먹으면	**meokda(ga)** 먹다(가)	**meokeotta(ga)** 먹었다(가)
wears on feet	**sin-** 신	**sineumyeon** 신으면	**sintta(ga)** 신다(가)	**sineotta(ga)** 신었다(가)
sits	**anj-** 앉	**anjeumyeon** 앉으면	**antta(ga)** 앉다(가)	**anjatta(ga)** 앉았다(가)
breaks	**busu-** 부수	**busumyeon-** 부수면	**buseotta(ga)** 부셨다(가)	**busyeotta(ga)** 부셨었다(가)

II. VOWEL BASES

rests	**swi-** 쉬	**swimyeon** 쉬면	**swida(ga)** 쉬다(가)	**swieotta(ga)** 쉬었다(가)
pays	**nae-** 내	**naemyeon** 내면	**naeda(ga)** 내다(가)	**naetta(ga)** 냈다(가)
writes	**sseu-** 쓰	**sseumyeon** 쓰면	**sseuda(ga)** 쓰다(가)	**sseotta(ga)** 썼다(가)
goes	**ga-** 가	**gamyeon** 가면	**gada(ga)** 가다(가)	**gatta(ga)** 갔다(가)
does	**ha-** 하	**hamyeon** 하면	**hada(ga)** 하다	**haetta(ga)** 했다(가)
calls	**bureu-** 부르	**bureumyeon** 부르면	**bureuda(ga)** 부르다(가)	**bulleotta(ga)** 불렀다(가)

III. -W BASES

MEANING	BASE	-EUMYEON, -MYEON	-DA(GA)	-ATTA(GA)
helps	**dow-**	**doumyeon**	**dopda(ga)**	**dowatta(ga)**
	도우	도우면	돕다 (가)	도왔다 (가)
lies down	**nuw-**	**nuumyeon**	**nupda(ga)**	**nuwotta(ga)**
	누우	누우면	눕다 (가)	누웠다 (가)
is near	**gakkaw-**	**kakkau-myeon**	**gakkapda (ga)**	**kakkawotta(ga)**
	가까우	가까우면	가깝다 (가)	가까웠다 (가)

IV. -R BASES

walks	**geor-**	**georeumyeon**	**geotta(ga)**	**georeotta(ga)**
	걸	걸으면	걷다 (가)	걸었다(가)
listens	**deur-**	**deureumyeon**	**deutta(ga)**	**deureotta(ga)**
	들	들으면	듣다 (가)	들었다(가)

V. L- EXTENDING VOWEL BASES

hangs	**geo-l-**	**geolmyeon**	**geolda(ga)**	**georeotta(ga)**
	걸	걸면	걸다 (가)	걸었다(가)
enters	**deu-l-**	**deureogamyeon**	**deureoga(ga)**	**deureogatta(ga)**
	들	들어가면	들어가다 (가)	들어갔다(가)

LESSON 42

Hoping and Wishing

To say *I hope something will happen* or *I wish something would happen* you use an expression which means literally *if something happens it will be nice* = **-eumyeon jokkesseoyo.**

Nun-i omyeon jokkesseoyo.
눈이 오면 좋겠어요.
I hope it snows.

Ilbon-edo ga bol ssu isseumyeon jokkesseoyo.
일본에도 가 볼 수 있으면 좋겠어요.
I hope I'll be able to go see Japan, too.

Hangungmal-eul Hanguk saram gachi jal hamyeon jokkesseoyo.
한국말을 한국사람같이 잘 하면 좋겠어요.
I wish I could speak Korean well like the Koreans.

Bi-ga an omyeon jokkesseoyo.
비가 안 오면 좋겠어요.
I hope it doesn't rain.

Uri jip-e osil ssu isseumyeon jokkesseoyo.
우리 집에 오실 수 있으면 좋겠어요.
It'll be nice if you can come to our house.

To say *I would like to do* you use **-go sipeoyo**:

Dosi-ro gago sipeoyo.

도시로 가고 싶어요.

I'd like to go to town.

To say *someone would like to do something* you say **-go sipeohaeyo**:

Eomma-ga swigo sipeohaeyo.

엄마가 쉬고 싶어해요.

Mother would like to rest.

But to say *someone would like* SOMEONE ELSE *to do something* you say **-hamyeon gomapgeseoyo.**

Muneul ryeoreojumyeon gomapgeseoyo.

문을 열어주면 고맙겠어요.

I'd appreciate if you open the door.

To GIVE permission you say **-eodo joa yo** (or **-eodo kwaen chanayo**) = *it is okay to, it is all right even if (you do)*.

To DENY permission, you use the expression **-eumyeon andweyo** = *it won't do to, one mustn't, oughtn't, shouldn't*. For the special meaning *won't do* you can use **mosseoyo** = *can't be used* instead of **an dweyo** = *does not become*:

Neukke omyeon an dweyo.

늦게오면 안돼요.

You mustn't come back late.

Aideul eun dambae pimyeon an dweyo.

아이들은 담배피면 안돼요.

Children shouldn't smoke cigarettes.

Hwanja hago orae malhamyeon an dweyo.

환자하고 오래 말하면 안돼요.

You mustn't talk with the patient long.

Sul-eul neomu mani masimyeon an dweyo.

술을 너무 많이 마시면 안돼요.

You shouldn't drink so (much).

Bi-ga omyeon sireoyo.

비가 오면 싫어요.

It's no good if it rains.

To say *has to, must* you use the expression **-eoya haeyo**.

But a milder way to expressing obligation is *ought* or *should* which the Koreans say with **-ji aneumyeon andweyo** = *if you don't, it's no good*:

Iljjik oji aneumyeon an dweyo.

일찍 오지 않으면 안돼요.

You should come back early.

Samusire jip-e gagi jeon-e bab-eul meogeoya haeyo.

사무실에 가기 전에 밥을 먹어야 해요.

I (we) have to eat before going to the office.

Gicha-ga tteonagi jeon-e eumsik-eul saya haeyo.

기차가 떠나기 전에 음식을 사야해요.

We ought to buy some food (stuffs) before the train leaves.

Eotteon geot-do manjeoseo-neun an dweyo.

어떤 것도 만져서는 안되요.

You ought not to touch anything.

What the Weather Looks Like

To say something *looks like* or *seems like* something you can use several expressions. One consists of any modifier form followed by **moyang ieyo** = *it's the appearance of.* Another consists of any modifier form followed by **geot gatayo** = *it's like the fact of.* The former expression stresses the appearance; the latter stresses the similarity:

Seonsaengnim cheoreom boyeoyo.
선생님처럼 보여요.
She looks like a teacher.

Seonsaengnim in geot gatayo.
선생님인 것 같아요.
She seems to be a teacher.

Here are some examples of these expressions:

Bi-ga ol geot gatayo.
비가 올 것 같아요.
It looks as if it will rain.

Eojet bam nun-i on geot gatayo.
어젯밤 눈이 온 것 같아요.
It looks as though it had snowed last night.

Nalssi-ga joeun geot gatayo.
날씨가 좋은 것 같아요.
The weather seems to be nice.

Nalssi-ga nabbeun geot gatayo.

날씨가 나쁜것 같아요.

The weather seems to be bad (nasty).

Haneul-e kureum-i isseoseo eoduweoyo.

하늘에 구름이 있어서 어두워요.

There are clouds in the sky, so it's dark.

Haneul-e gureum-i isseoseo eodupjiman, hae-ga naogo isseoyo.

하늘에 구름이 있어서 어둡지만 해가 나오고 있어요.

There are clouds in the sky, so it's dark, but it looks like the sun is coming out.

Hae-ga nawaseo balgayo.

해가 나와서 밝아요.

The sun is out, so it's light.

Oneul achim-e baram-i buna bwayo?

오늘 아침에 바람이 부나 봐요.

Does there seem to be a wind blowing this morning?

Adeul-i bus-reul nocheosseul ji-do molayo.

아들이 버스를 놓쳤을지도 몰라요.

My son seems to have missed the bus.

To say that something *gets to be, turns into* a certain condition, you use the infinitive of an adjective followed by the auxiliary verb **joayo** (base **ji-**).

Deowojeosseoyo.

더워졌어요.

It's gotten hot.

Deowoyo.

더워요.

It is hot.

Siwon haejimyeon doragal geyo.

시원해지면 돌아갈게요.

I'll go back when it gets cool.

Siwonhan got-eul chakko isseoyo.

시원한 곳을 찾고 있어요.

I'm looking for a cool spot.

Hae-ga tteumyeon, deowojyeoyo.

해가 뜨면 더워져요.

When the sun comes out, it gets warm.

Yeogi-ga ttatteut hago joayo.

여기가 따뜻하고 좋아요.

This place is nice and warm.

Neomu deowojjiman chukku hareo nagasseoyo.

너무 더웠지만 축구하러 나갔어요.

It was hot, but I went out to play soccer.

Because

You have learned that **-eoseo** links two verbal expressions stressing that the second is the consequence of the first: *and so*. This is a very weak way of saying the second expression *is so* BECAUSE of the first. There are a number of ways in which this BECAUSE can be made a bit stronger.

The most common is to use the **-gi** form followed by **ttaemun-(e)**:

Bi-ga ogi ttaemune nagago sipji anayo.
비가 오기 때문에 나가고 싶지 않아요.
I don't want to go because it's raining.

Doni eopgi ttaemune eommaneun nagago sipji anayo.
돈이 없기 때문에 엄마는 나가고 싶지 않아요.
Mom doesn't want to go out because she doesn't have any money.

For the past and future there are special forms which consist of inserting the past marker (**-eoss-** in its basic form) or the future marker (**-kesse-** in its basic form) between the base and **-gi**: **-eokki** (**-akki**, etc.) and **-gekki**.

Meonjeo bap-eul meogeoseo baegopeuji anayo.
먼저 밥을 먹어서 배 고프지 않아요.
I'm not hungry because I've already eaten.

Nae-ga naeil Gim seonsaeng-eul mannagi ttaemun-e, geu bun-hante geu iyagi-reul hal geyo.
내가 내일 김 선생을 만나기 때문에 그 분한테 그 이야기를 할게요.
I'll tell Mr. Kim about that, because I'll see him tomorrow.

Wae geureoke neukke doraoseyo?

왜 그렇게 늦게 돌아오세요?

Why do you come home so late?

Gongjang-eseo haeya hal il-i neomu manaseoyo.

공장에서 해야 할 일이 너무 많아서요.

It's because we had a lot of work to do at the factory.

Another way to say *because* is to use a modifier form followed by **kkadalk** = *reason*. This may be followed by **e** or **euro** with about the same meaning *for the reason that* or by **ieyo** with the meaning *it is for the reason that, it is because*:

Nun-i neomu mani omyeon unjeon hagi him deureoyo.

눈이 너무 많이 오면 운전하기 힘 들어요.

We can't drive the car because it is snowing so hard.

Uri-ga georeo gaya haeseo neujeul geo eyo.

우리가 걸어가야 해서 늦을 거에요.

We'll arrive late because we'll have to walk.

Il-eul mani haekki ttaemun-e pigon haeyo.

일을 많이 했기 때문에 피곤해요.

I'm tired because I had to work a lot.

Wae geu sonyeo reul joahaseyo? Geu sonyeo ga yeppeo seoyo?

왜 그 소녀를 좋아하세요? 그 소녀가예뻐서요?

Why do you like that girl? Is it because she has a pretty face (.... her face is pretty)?

Casual Remarks Using *-ji yo*

You have learned that the **-ji** form appears in negative sentences (**-jianayo** = *does not, is not*) and at the end of clauses with the particle **man** (**-jiman** = *does but, is but*).

This form also appears at the end of a sentence before the polite particle **yo**. The meaning of a sentence ending in **-jiyo** is about the same as one ending in **-eoyo**—this is just a more CASUAL way of putting the sentence. These casual sentences are frequently mixed with ordinary sentences and sometimes the casual flavor gives them rather special meanings. For one thing, these are about the only sentences that occur with that peculiar dipping intonation you may have noticed with the expression **Aniyo** = *No*.

The meaning of this dipping intonation is to LIVEN UP the sentence or to INSIST ON it; often the sentence is a sort of question, and the meaning is *…it is, isn't it?* or *does, doesn't it?*:

Gim seonsaeng isi jiyo?
김 선생이시지요?
You are Mr. Kim, aren't you?

Yeogi-seo jom swieodo dwejiyo?
여기서 좀 쉬어도 되지요?
It'll be all right to rest here a bit, won't it?

Often the **-jiyo** form is a COMMAND or PROPOSITION, offered somewhat casually. This is especially frequent when the verb is honorific:

Cha han jan masilkkayo?
차 한 잔 마실까요?
Shall we have a cup of tea?

Cha han jan masipsida.
차 한 잔 마십시다.
Let's have a cup of tea.

Iri oseyo.
이리 오세요.
Come this way.

Yeogi anjeuseyo.
여기 앉으세요.
Sit here.

Jamkkan gidaryeo juseyo.
잠깐 기다려 주세요.
Wait just a moment.

Yeonghwa boreo galkkayo?
영화보러 갈까요?
Shall we go to a movie?

Yeonghwa boreo gapsida.
영화보러 갑시다.
Let's see a movie.

Sometimes the **-jiyo** form is a question, again rather casual:

Myeotsie doraosijiyo?
몇 시에 돌아오시지요?
What time will you be back?

Miguk-e eonje doragasi jiyo?
미국에 언제 돌아 가시지요?
When will you be going back to America?

If the **-ji** form is a statement about someone else, the English translation can suggest the flavor of the casualness by adding a rather meaningless *you know* or *don't you know* or *I guess*.

Often this is a way of GIVING INFORMATION in Korean—the casualness has a polite tinge:

Dangsin-do asijiman Miguk-edo chuun nal-i ijjiyo.
당신도 아시지만 미국에도 추운 날이 있지요.
We have cold days (or weather) in America too, you know.

Beuraun sowiga Sikago eseo sal jiyo.
브라운 소위가 시카코에서 살지요.
Mr. Brown lives in Chicago.

Na-neun euisa-ga anigo ganhosa ijiyo.
나는 의사가 아니라 간호사이지요.
I'm not a doctor, you know. I'm a nurse you see.

Geu seonsaengnim-eun Hanguk saram ieyo?
그 선생님은 한국 사람이지요?
Is that teacher a Korean?

Mullon ijiyo!
물론이지요.
Of course!

You do not usually answer questions about yourself with the **-jiyo** form. Use the ordinary **eoyo** form instead.

Some Abbreviations

Here are some common shortened forms. **Geot** is shortened to **geo**, **geot-i** to **ge**, and **geot ieyo** to **geyo**. **Ige nae kkeo eyo** = **Igeot-i nae-kkeo eyo**. *This is mine.*

Mueot is shortened to **mweo** or **meo**, **mueot-i** to **m(u)e** and **mueot ieyo** to **m(u)e yo**. **M(u)et isseoyo?** = **Mueot-i isseoyo?** *What do you have?* **M(u)e yo?** = **Mueosieyo?** *What is it?*

The particle **neun** is abbreviated to **n** after a vowel: **na n** = **na-neun** = *as for me*, **igeon** = **igeot-eun** = *this thing*. The particle **reul** is abbreviated to **l** after a vowel: **nal** = **na reul** = *me* (as direct object), **igeol** = **igeot-eul** = *this thing* (as direct object).

You have already learned that **nugu** becomes **nu** in front of the particle **ga**, and that **na** becomes **nae** in that position. And you have learned that **ani** is shortened to **an** in front of a verb. You may run into other abbreviations from time to time; try to find out what the full form of the abbreviation is. If you show you haven't understood, a Korean will repeat himself and often give you an expanded version of an abbreviated expression just as we often repeat *do not* for *don't* when we slow down.

The Stucture of Verb Forms

A complete description of Korean verbs is too involved for a textbook of this size. However, a general notion of the structure of the forms may be of help to you. Look at the following table which shows, in a rough way, how the verb forms are put together.

1	2	3	4	5	6	(7)
BASE	HONORIFIC	PAST	PAST	FUTURE	MOOD	(PARTICLE)
	-(eu)s(i)-	-ass-	-ass-	-gess-	-eo, -a, -e	(yo)
		-ass-			-hal-	
		etc.				
					-go	
					-gi	
					-chi	
					-(eu)myeon	
					etc.	

Now look at the forms below:

1	2	3	4	5	6	(7)
dad-					-eo	(yo)
dat-				-gess-	-eo	(yo)
dad-		-ass-			-eo	(yo)
dad-	-eus-				-eo	(yo)
dad-		-ass-			-eo	(yo)
dad-		-ad-	eul	-geo-	-eo	(yo)
dad-		-ass-	-eul-	-geo-	-eo	(yo)
dad-	-eus	-i		-gess-	-eo	(yo)

BASE	HONORIFIC	PAST	PAST	FUTURE	MOOD	(PARTICLE)
dad-	**-eus-**	**-yeoss-**			**-eo**	**(yo)**
dad-	**-eus-**	**-yeoss-**	**-eoss-**		**-eo**	**(yo)**
dad-	**-eus-**	**-eot-**		**-gess-**	**-eo**	**(yo)**
dad-	**-eus-**	**-yeot-**	**-eot-**	**-ge-**	**-ji**	**(yo)**

These forms have the following meanings:

Dadayo.
닫아요.
Closes.

Dakkesseoyo.
닫겠어요.
Will close. Probably closes.

Dadasseoyo.
닫았어요.
Closed.

Dadeuseyo.
닫으세요.
Someone honored closes.

Dadaseoseoyo.
닫았었어요.
Had closed. Closed.

Dadeul geoeyo.
닫을 거에요.
Will close; probably closes.

Dadasseul geoeyo.
닫았을 거에요.
Will have closed. Probably had closed.

Dadeusigesseoyo.

닫으시겠어요.

Someone honored will close. Someone honored probably closes.

Dadeusyeosseoyo.

닫으셨어요.

Someone honored closed.

Dadeu syoesseosseoyo.

닫으셨었어요.

Someone honored had closed.

Dadeu syeosseul geoeyo.

닫으셨을 거에요.

Someone honored will have closed. Someone honored probably closed.

Dadeusyeokket jiyo.

닫으셨겠지요.

Someone honored will have closed. Someone honored probably had closed.

The past-past (*had done, did*) and the past-future (*will have done, probably did*) are not often used.

There are quite a lot of *moods* (the final suffix in the verb form) and you have only learned a few of the most useful ones in this book.

Romanization Table

The following Romanization table compares the transliteration of the USUAL or BASIC values of the Korean letters. There are six columns.

The first shows the letter of the Korean alphabet, **Hangeul**. These are arranged not according to any traditional order, but according to their phonetic characteristics.

The second column presents the standard Korean government romanization system which was introduced in the year 2000 and is used throughout this book.

The third column presents the McCune-Reischauer transcription.

The fourth column shows the Yale Romanization used by the author in other publications on the Korean language. This system avoids the use of unusual symbols or gadgets over ordinary letters by taking advantage of certain principles built into the structure of the language. But it takes a little while to get used to the values of some of the spellings.

The fifth column gives the Romanization used by Fred Lukoff in his textbook *Spoken Korean* (2 vols, Henry Holt and Company). This book contains a lot of excellent conversation practice and you might want to continue your study of Korean with it.

The last column shows the symbols used by Elinor Clark Horne in her book *Introduction to Spoken Korean* (2 vols., Far Eastern Publications, Yale University). This book is no longer in print.

Learning the shapes of native Korean symbols is just part of the job in learning to read and write; you will also need to know something about Korean spelling rules and the ways the symbols are put together to make syllables and words. Koreans will be glad to help you with this once you have learned something of the spoken language.

Hangeul	New romanization	McCune-R.	Yale	Lukoff	Horne
ㅂ	p, b	p, b	p	p	p
ㅍ	p	p'	ph	ph	ph, pph
ㅃ	pp	pp	pp	pp	pp
ㄷ	d	t, d	t	t	t
ㅌ	t	t'	th	th	th, tth
ㄸ	tt	tt	tt	tt	tt
ㅅ	s	s	s	s	s
ㅆ	ss	ss	ss	ss	ss
ㅈ	j	ch, j	c	j	c
ㅊ	ch	ch'	ch	jh	ch, tch
ㅉ	jj	tch	cc	jj	tc
ㄱ	g, k	k, g	k	k	k
ㅋ	k	k'	kh	kh	kh, kkh
ㄲ	kk	kk	kk	kk	kk
ㅁ	m	m	m	m	m
ㄴ	n	n	n	n	n
ㅇ	ng	ng	ng	ng	ŋ
ㄹ	r, l	r, l	l	l	l
ㅎ	h	h	h	h	h
ㅣ	i	i	i	i	i
ㅟ	wi	wi	wi	wi	wi
ㅔ	e	e	ey	e	e
ㅖ	ye	ye	yey	ye	ye
ㅞ	we	we	wey	we	we
ㅚ	ui	oe	oy	ö	we
ㅐ	ae	ae	ay	ä	ɛ
ㅒ	yae	yae	yay	yä	yɛ
ㅙ	wae	wae	way	wä	wɛ
ㅡ	eu	ŭ	u	tt	ə
ㅓ	eo	ŏ	e	ø	ɔ
ㅕ	yeo	yŏ	ye	yø	yɔ
ㅝ	wo	wŏ	we	wø	wɔ
ㅏ	a	a	a	a	a
ㅑ	ya	ya	ya	ya	ya
ㅘ	wa	wa	wa	wa	wa
ㅜ	u	u	*wu	u	u
ㅠ	yu	yu	yu	yu	yu
ㅗ	o	o	o	o	o
ㅛ	yo	yo	yo	yo	yo
ㅢ	ui	ŭi	uy	tt, i tti	əi

* but **u** after **p, ph, pp, m, y**